AGILITY

Faults and Foibles

by James Liddle

Howln Moon Press
Franklin, New York

Agility Faults and Foibles

Written and Illustrated by James Liddle ©2006

Printed and bound in the United States of America

ISBN 1-888994-24-X

Published by Howln Moon Press
7222 State Highway 357
Franklin, New York 13775
607-829-2187

Heartfelt thanks to all my fans who enjoy a good laugh!

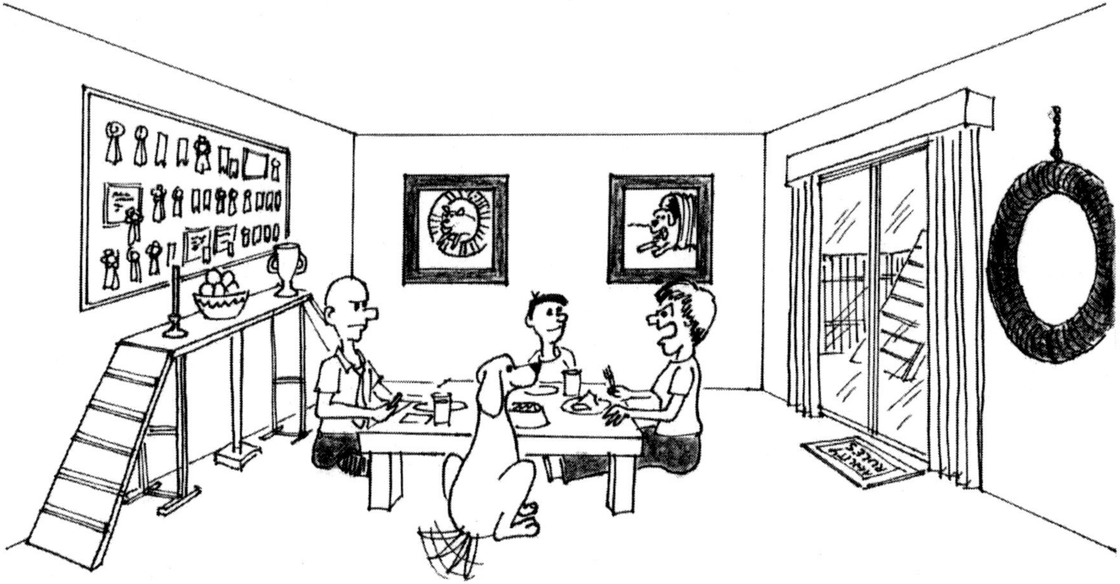

AGILITY HAS <u>NOT</u> TAKEN OVER OUR LIVES!

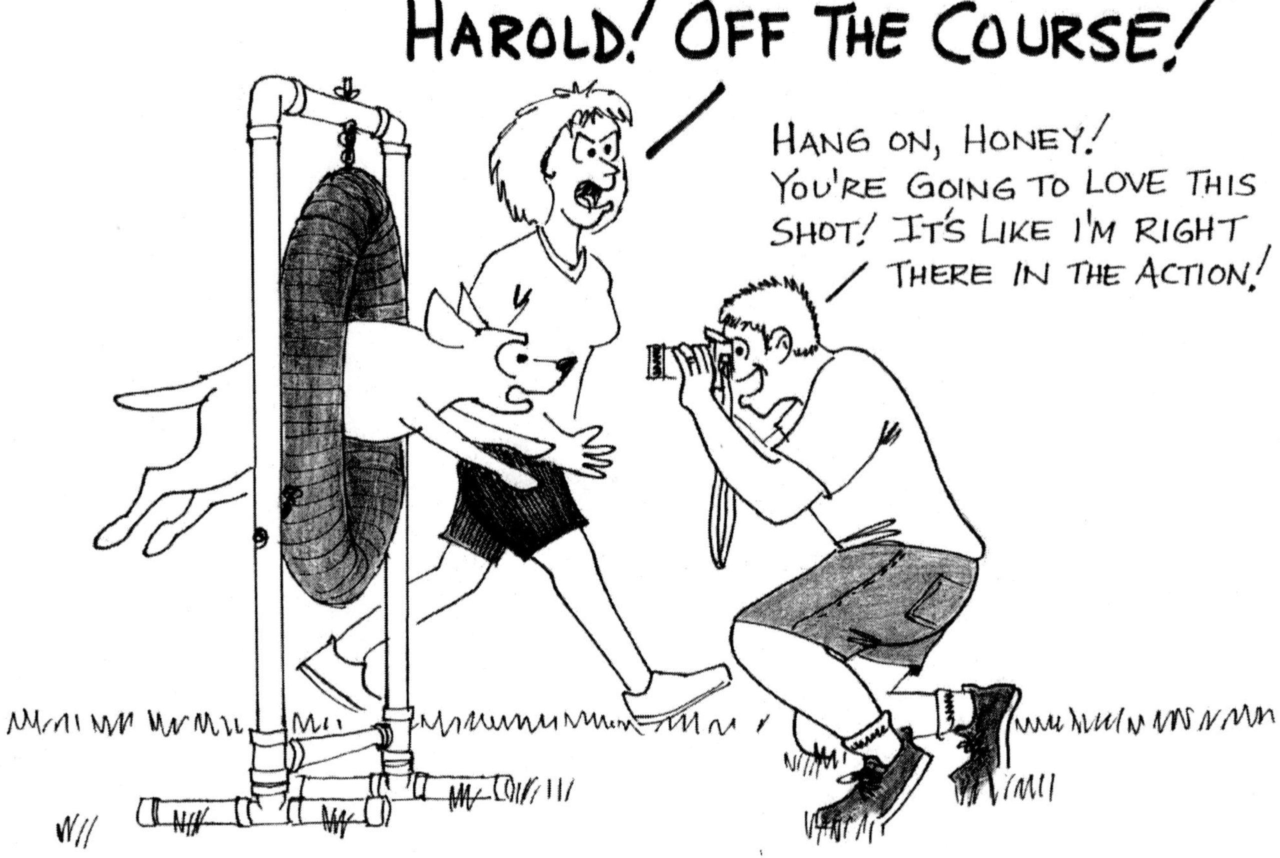
HAROLD! OFF THE COURSE!
HANG ON, HONEY! YOU'RE GOING TO LOVE THIS SHOT! IT'S LIKE I'M RIGHT THERE IN THE ACTION!

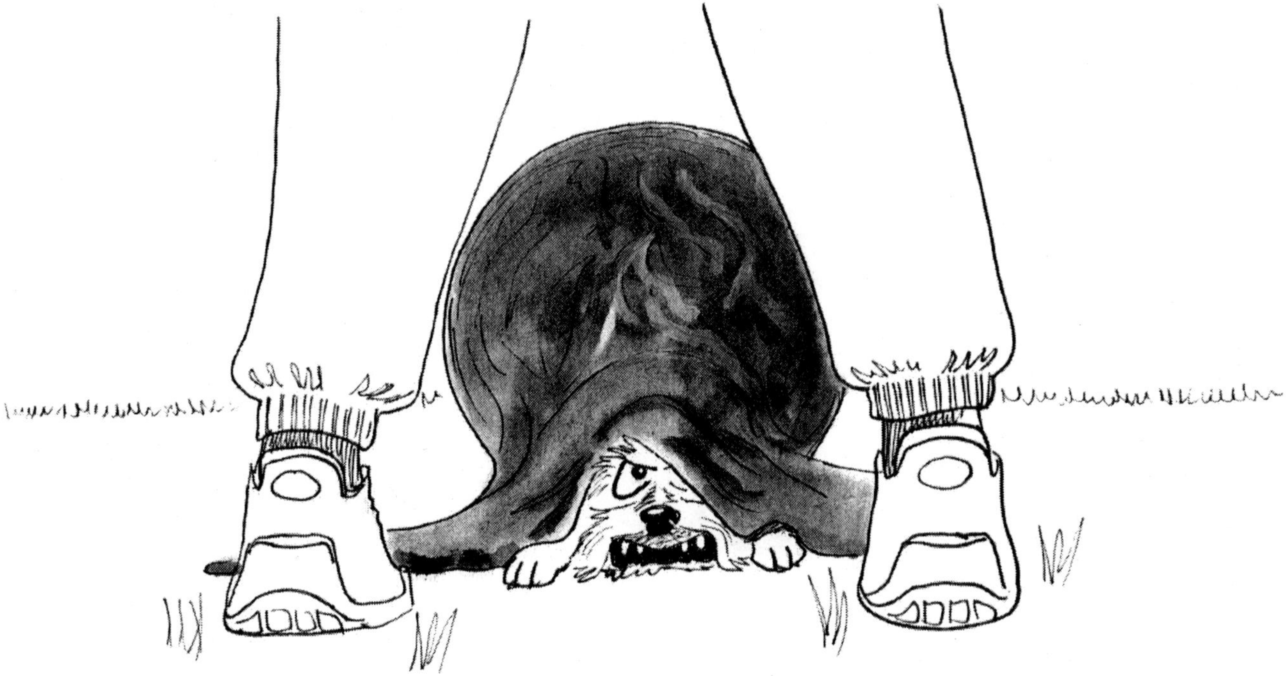

IS THAT BAD WIDDLE CHUTE TOO HEAVY FOR YOU?

THIS TUNNEL

RIGHT HERE!

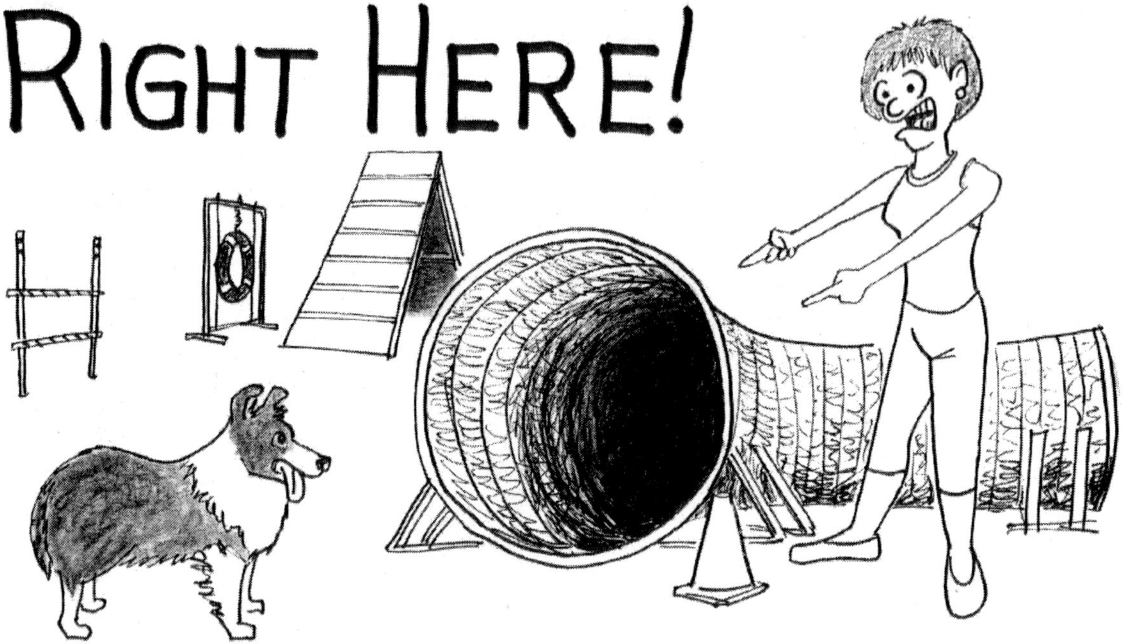

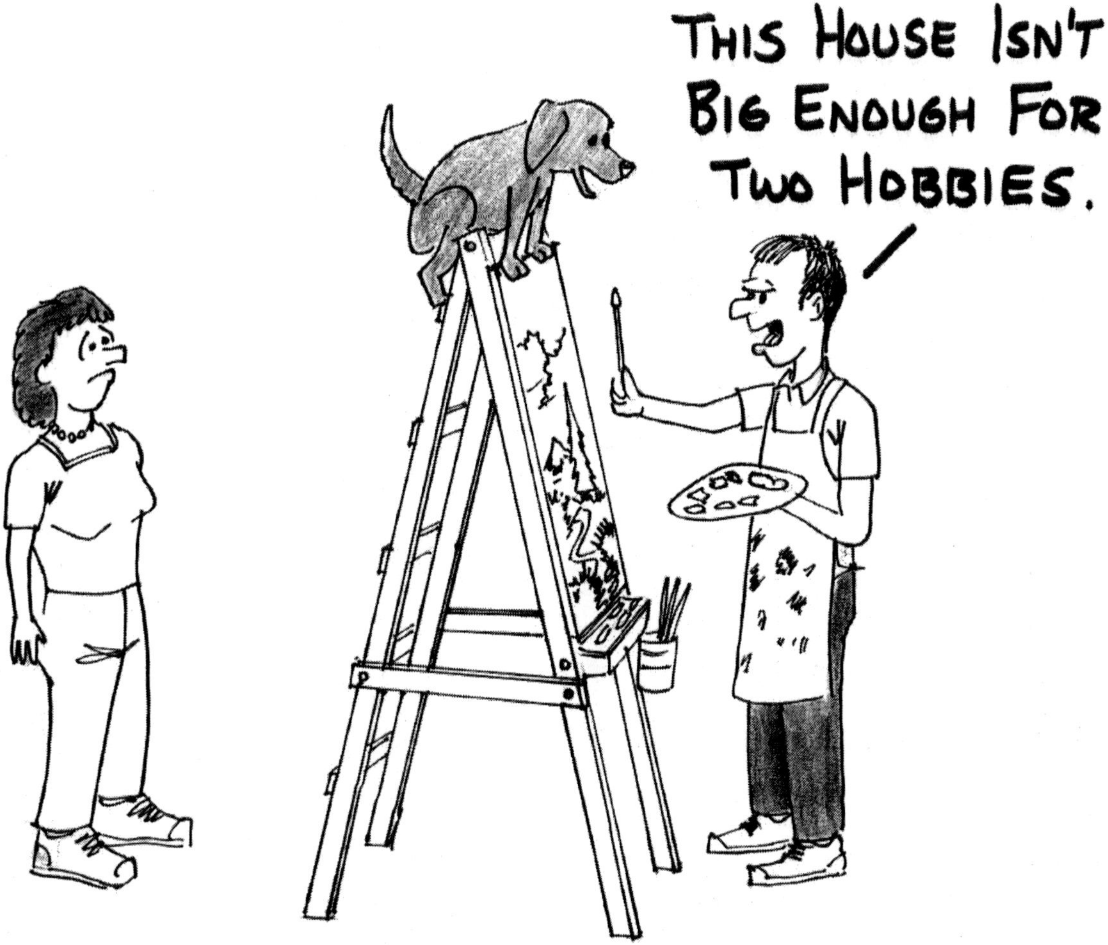
THIS HOUSE ISN'T BIG ENOUGH FOR TWO HOBBIES.

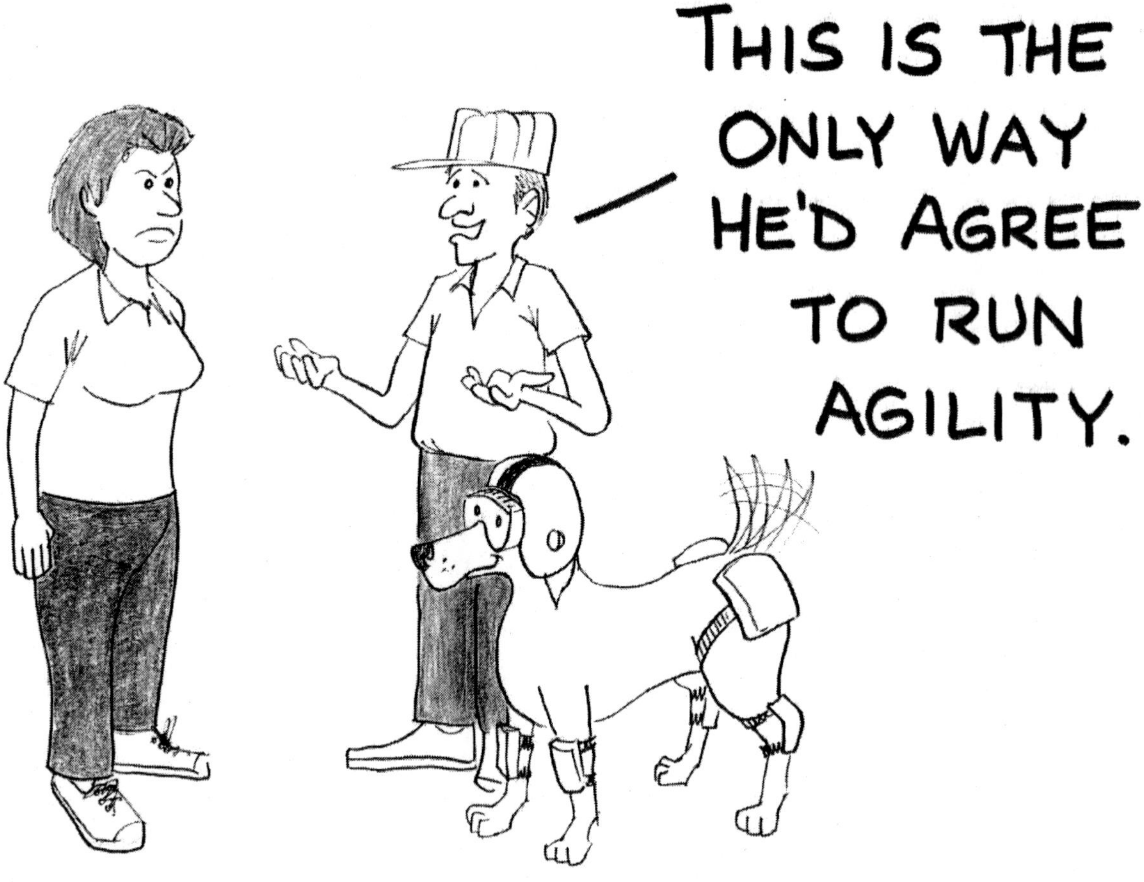
THIS IS THE ONLY WAY HE'D AGREE TO RUN AGILITY.

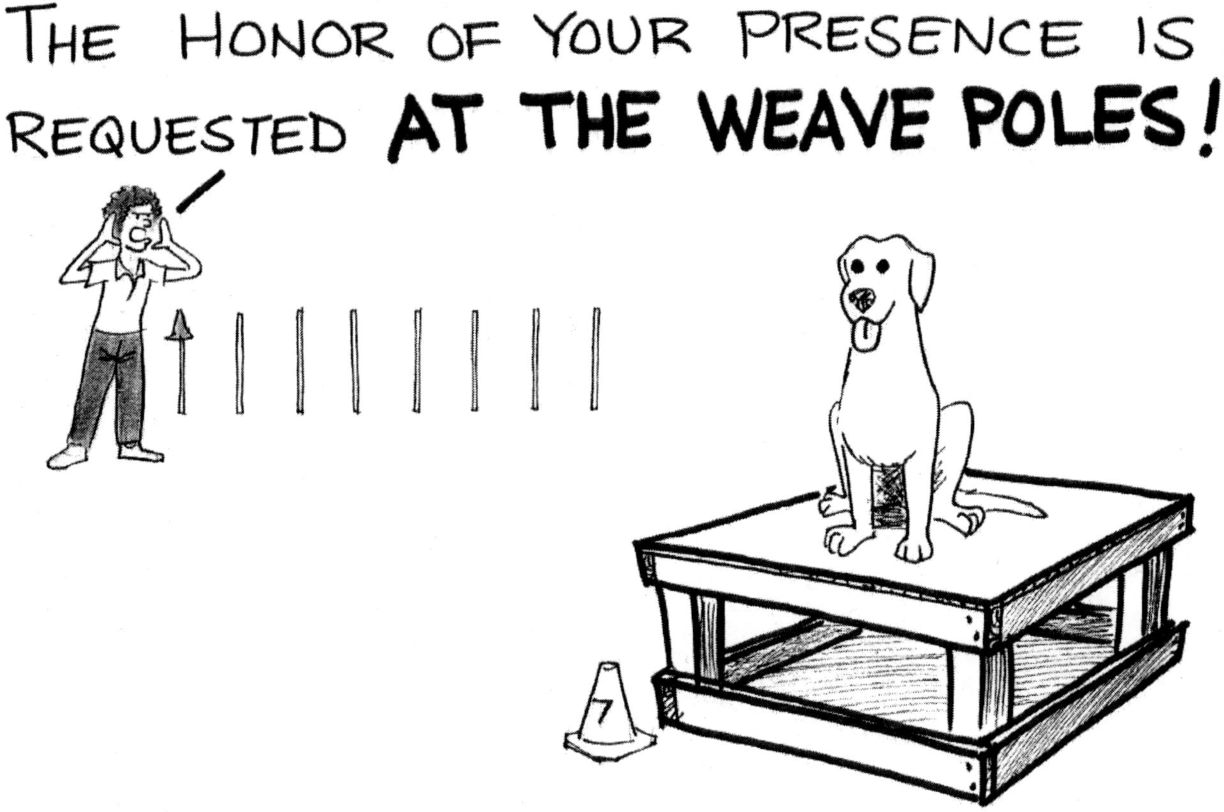
THE HONOR OF YOUR PRESENCE IS REQUESTED AT THE WEAVE POLES!
7

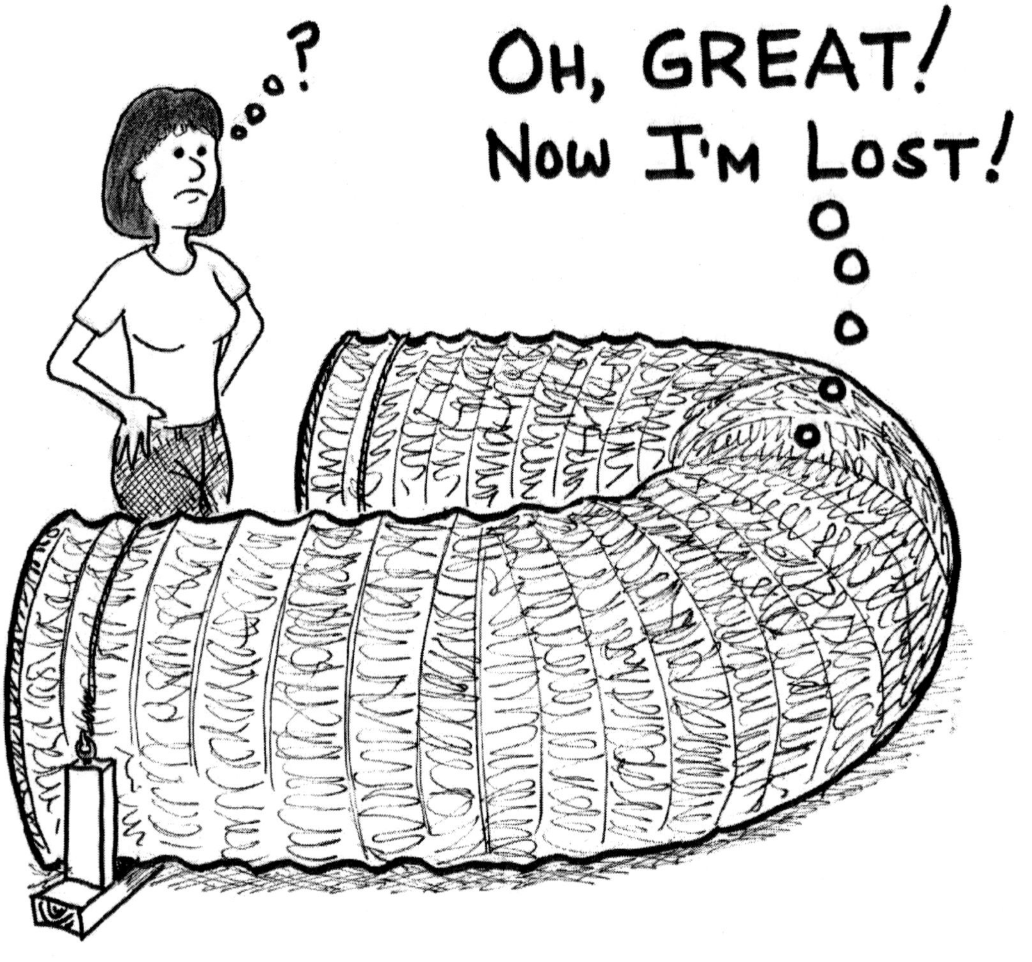
?
OH, GREAT!
NOW I'M LOST!

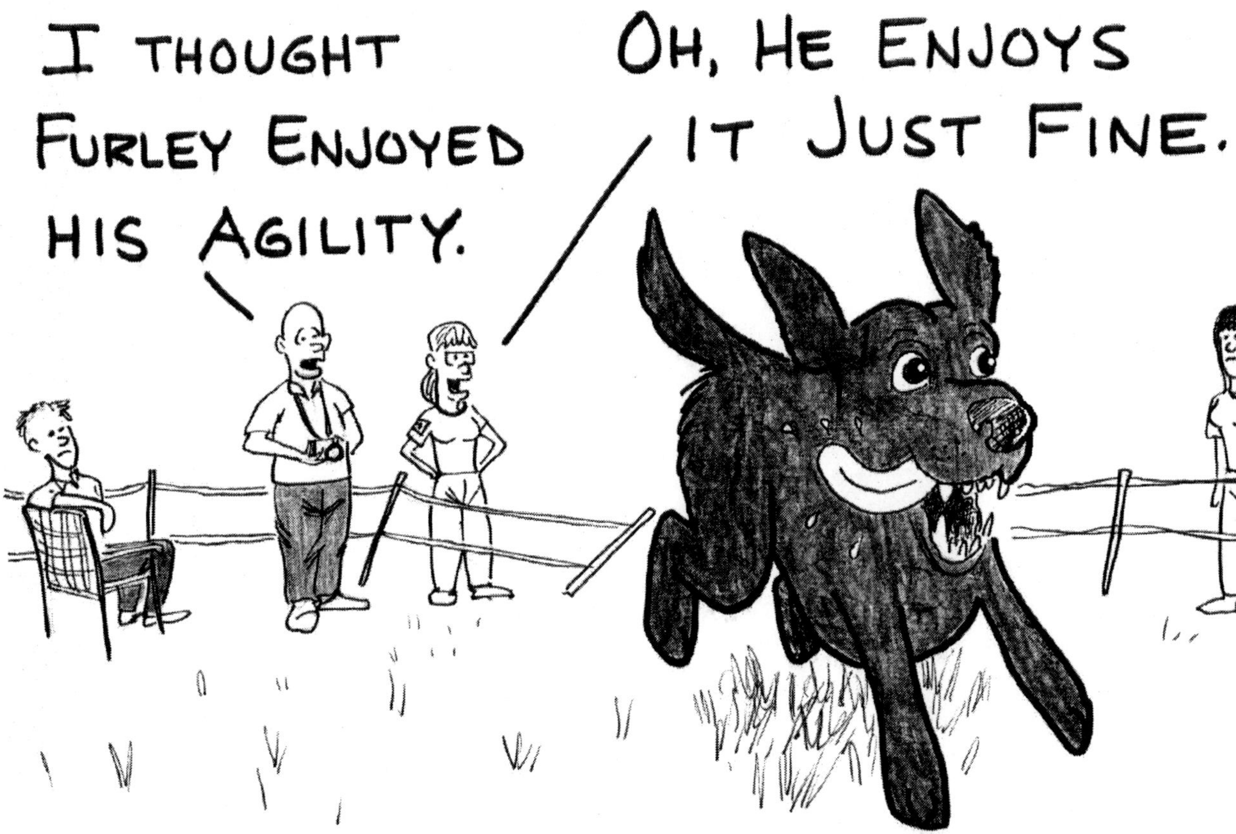
I THOUGHT FURLEY ENJOYED HIS AGILITY.
OH, HE ENJOYS IT JUST FINE.

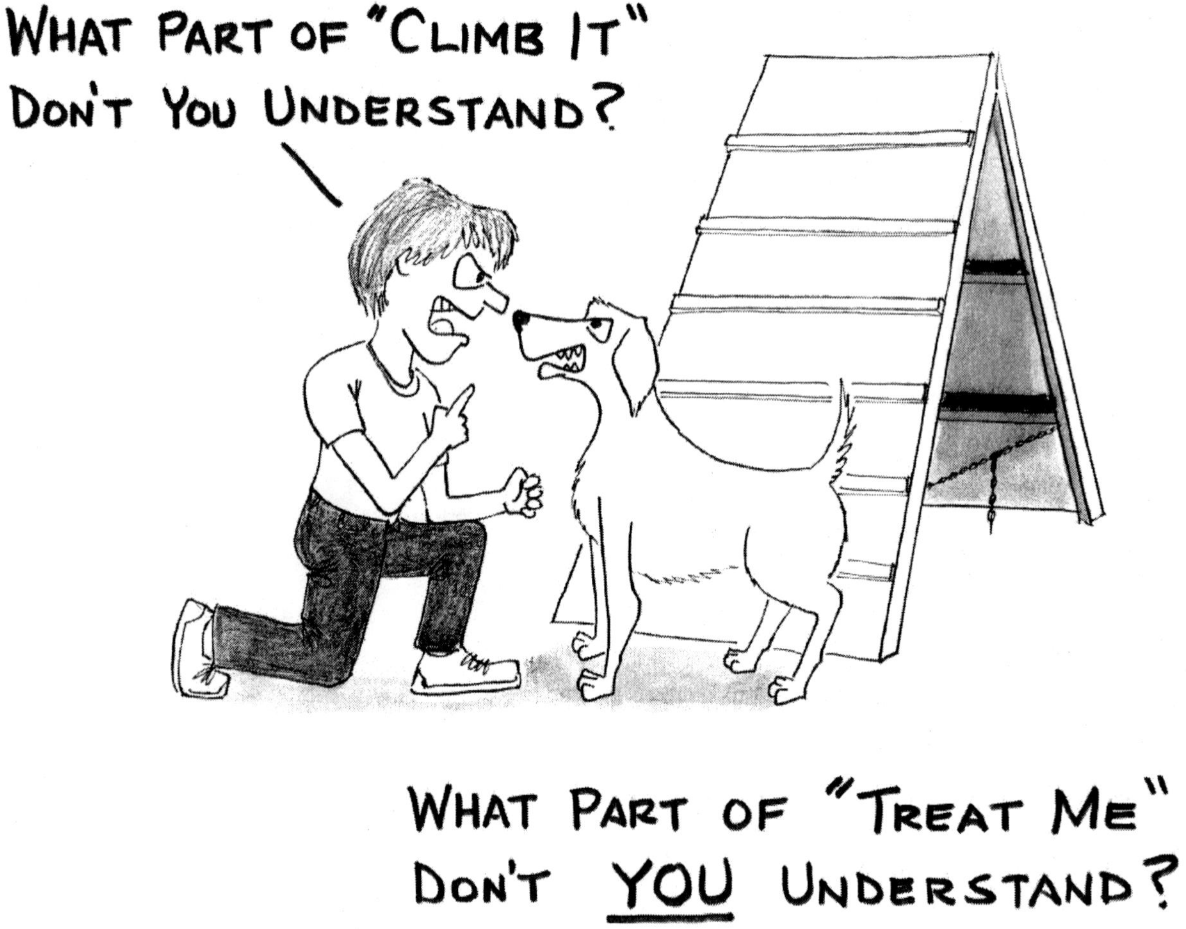
WHAT PART OF "CLIMB IT" DON'T YOU UNDERSTAND?
WHAT PART OF "TREAT ME" DON'T YOU UNDERSTAND?

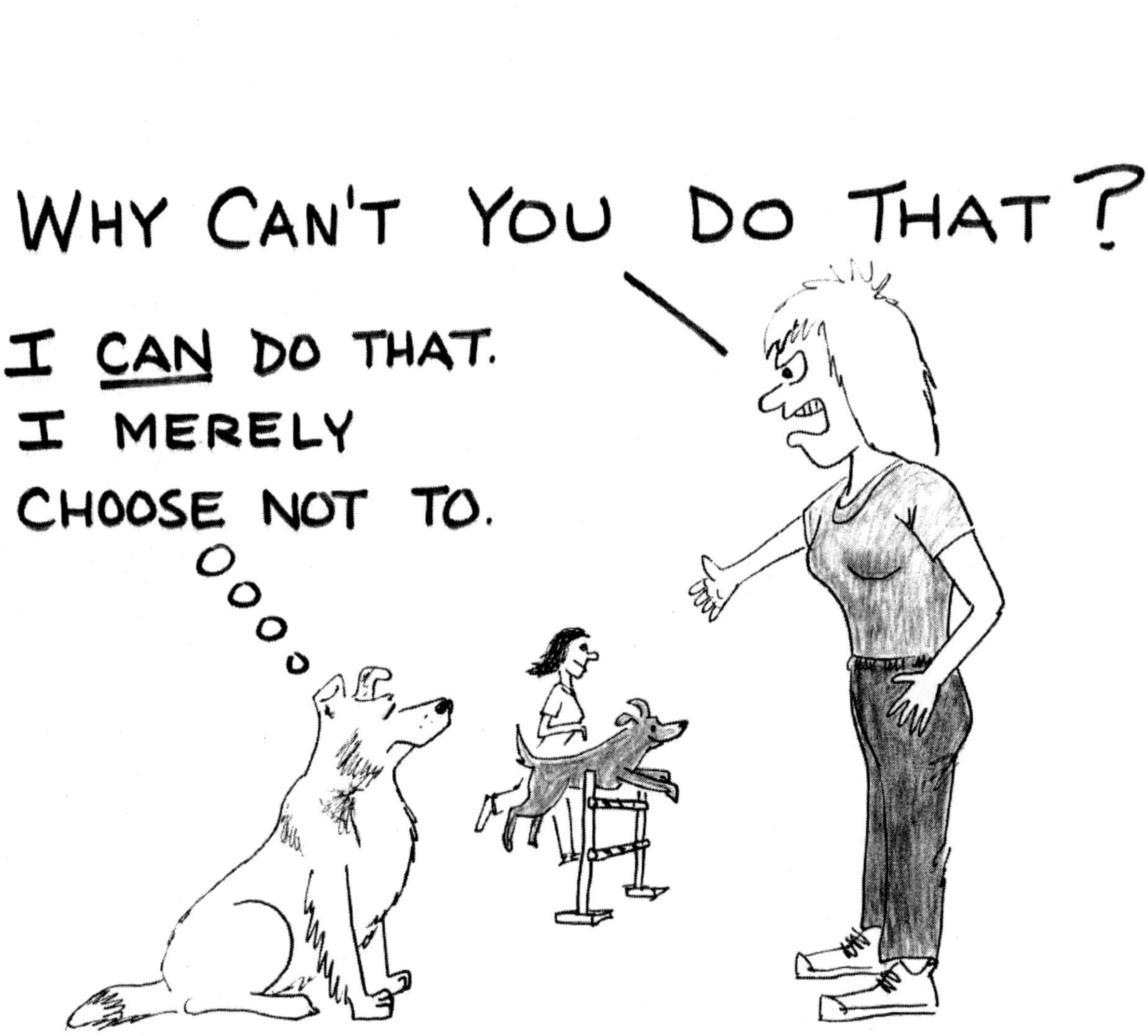
WHY CAN'T YOU DO THAT?
I CAN DO THAT. I MERELY CHOOSE NOT TO.

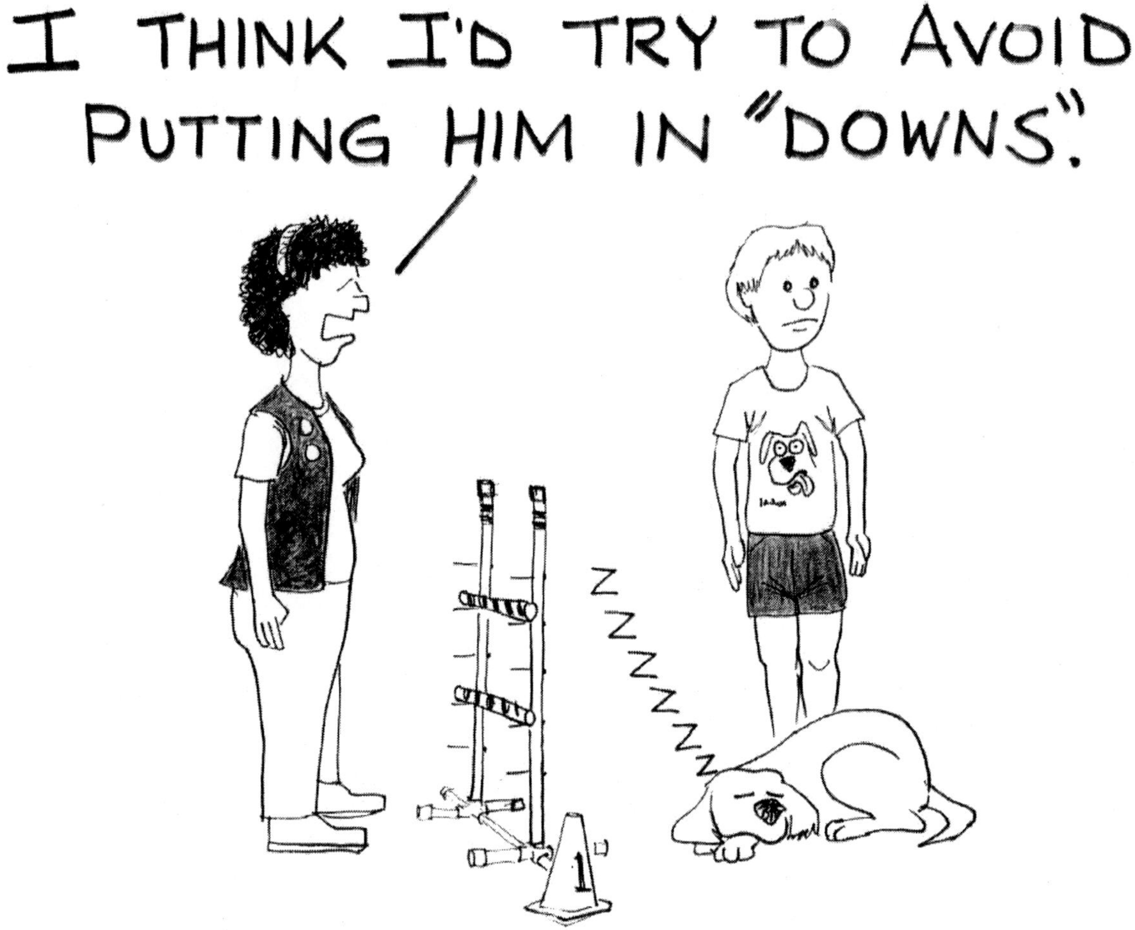
I THINK I'D TRY TO AVOID PUTTING HIM IN "DOWNS".
ZZZZZZZ

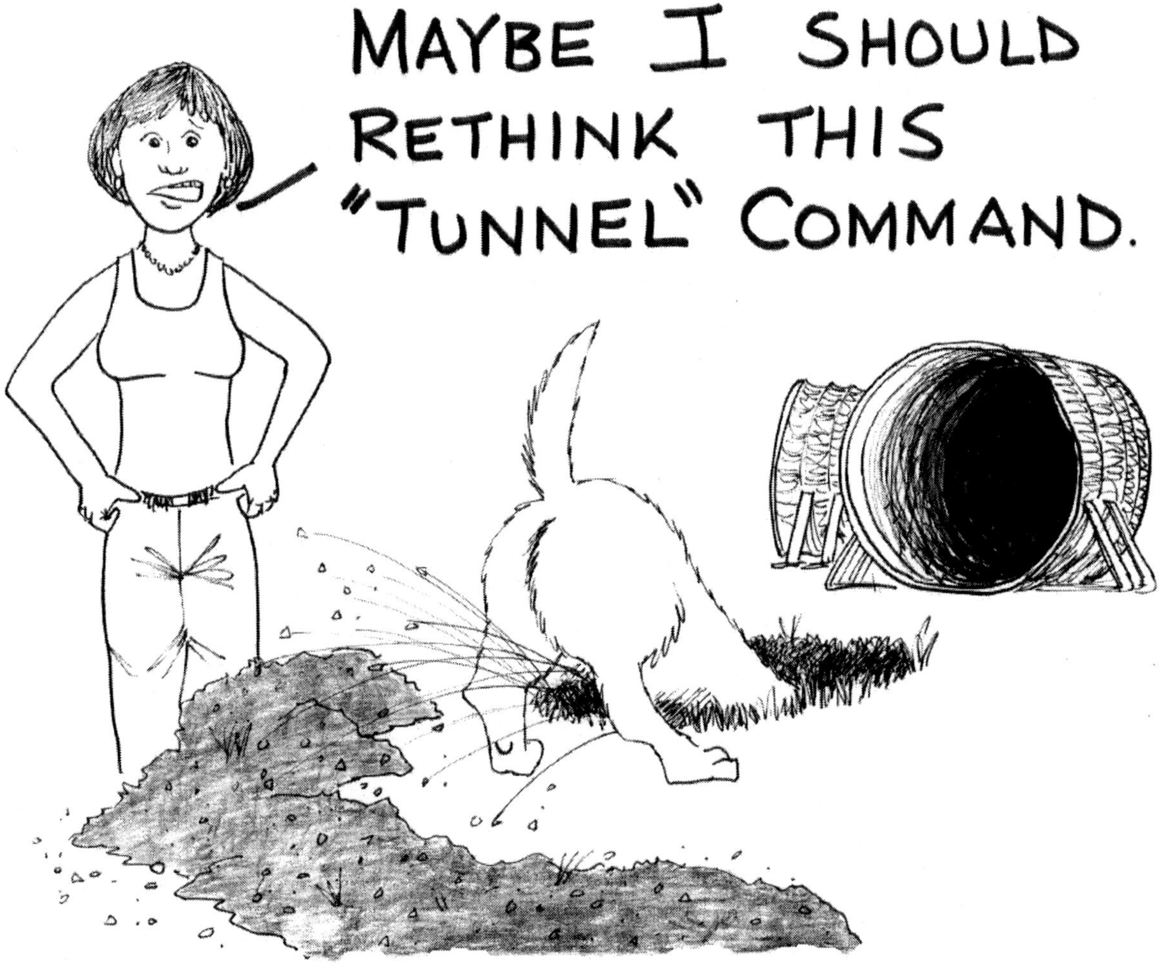
MAYBE I SHOULD RETHINK THIS "TUNNEL" COMMAND.

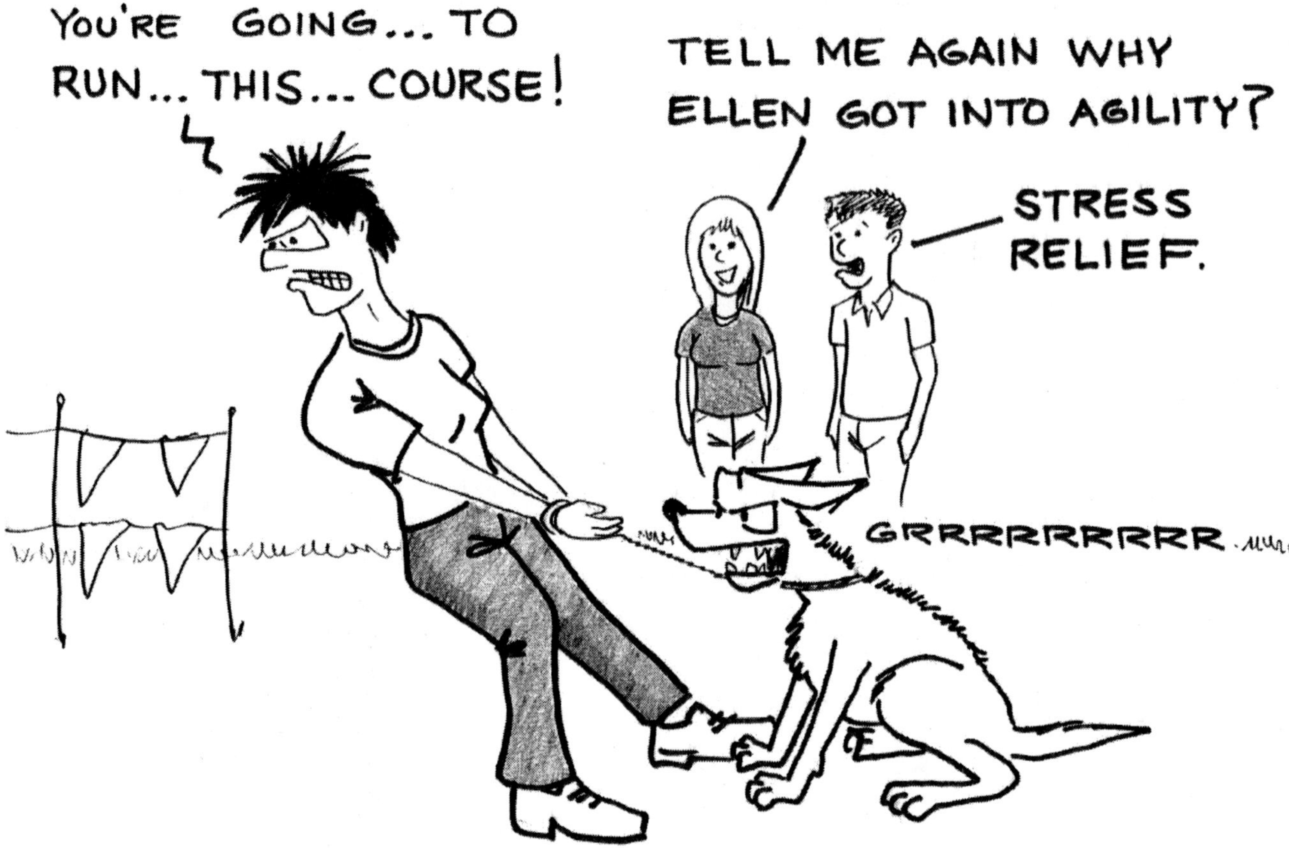
YOU'RE GOING... TO RUN... THIS... COURSE!
TELL ME AGAIN WHY ELLEN GOT INTO AGILITY?
STRESS RELIEF.
GRRRRRRRRRR

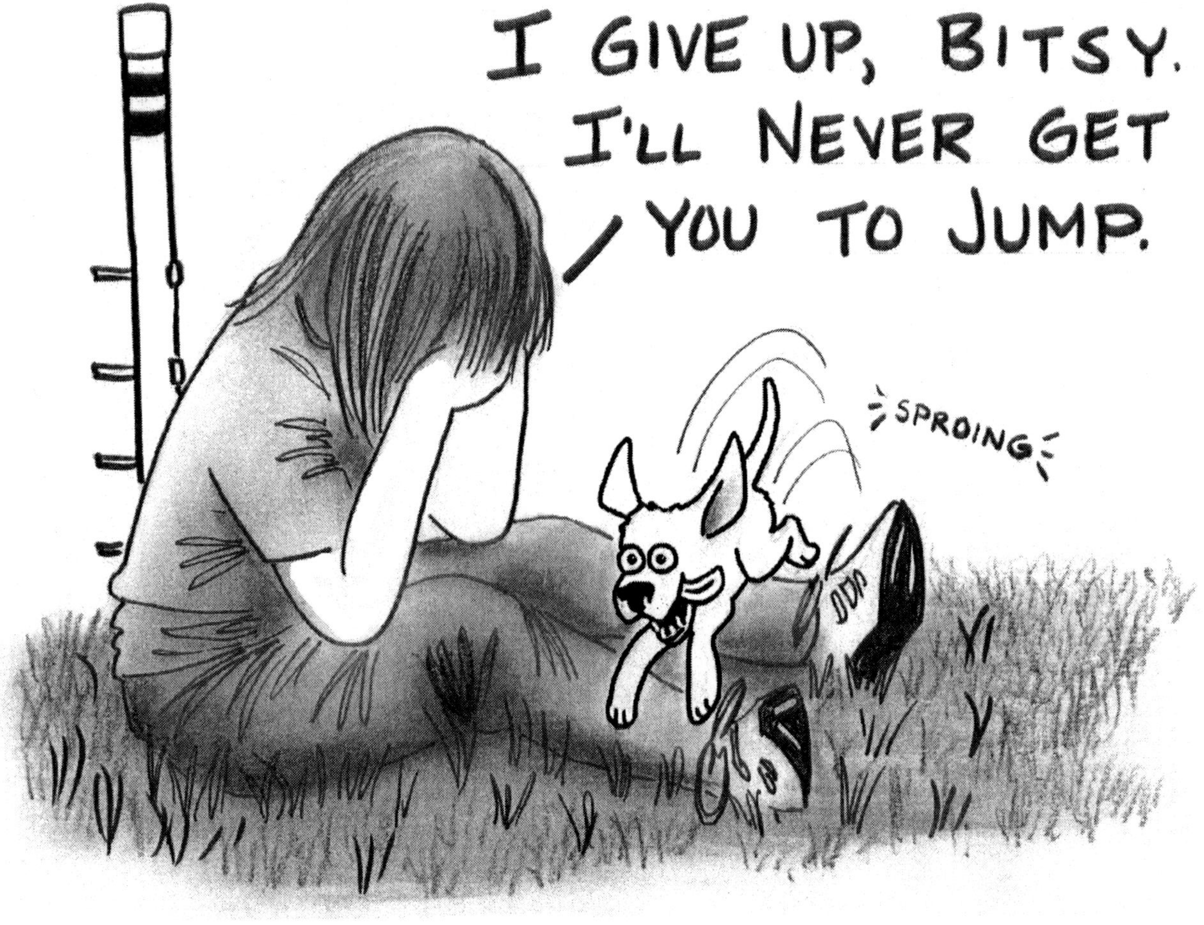
I GIVE UP, BITSY. I'LL NEVER GET YOU TO JUMP.
SPROING

I THINK IT'S SAFE TO SAY THAT WE'RE OVER OUR TIME LIMIT.

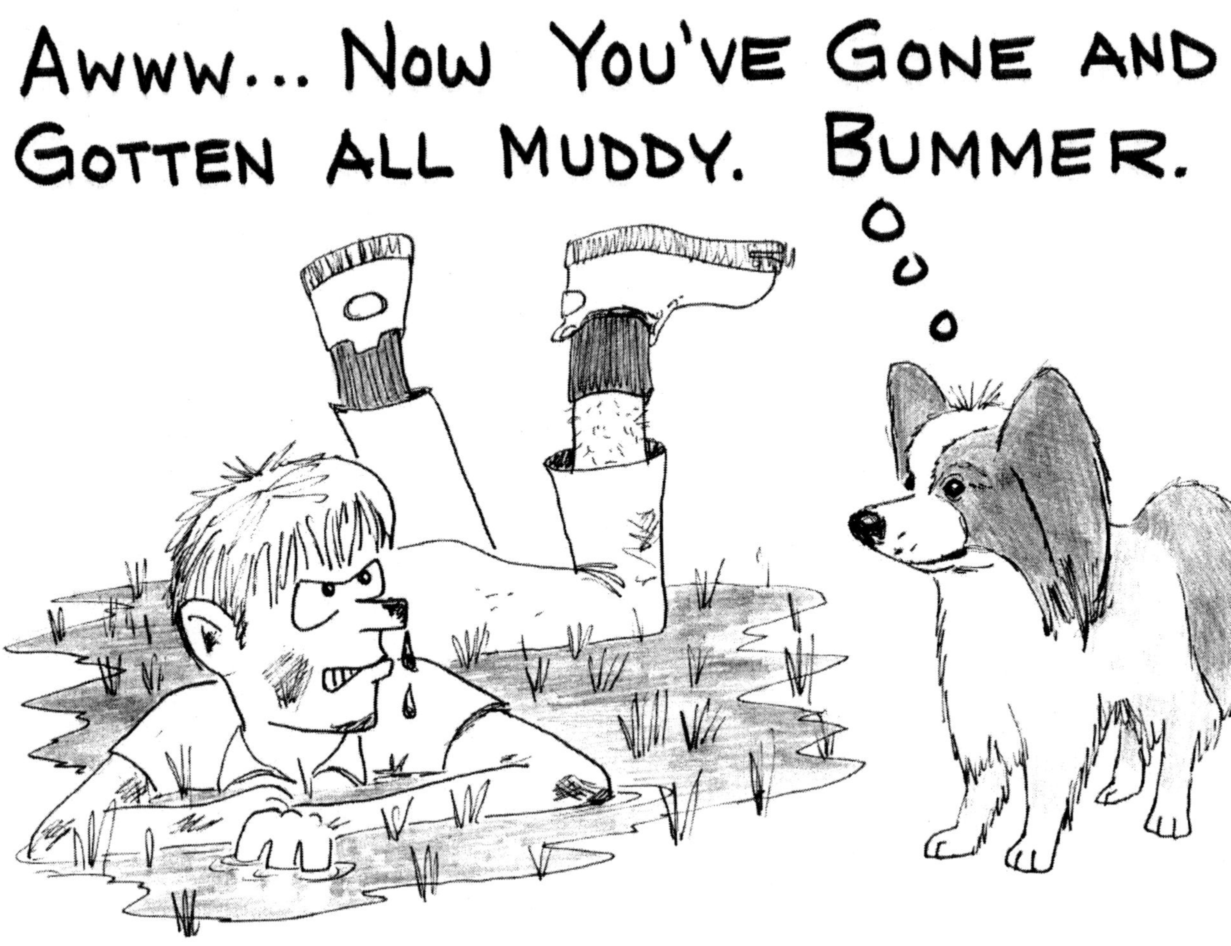
AWWW... NOW YOU'VE GONE AND GOTTEN ALL MUDDY. BUMMER.

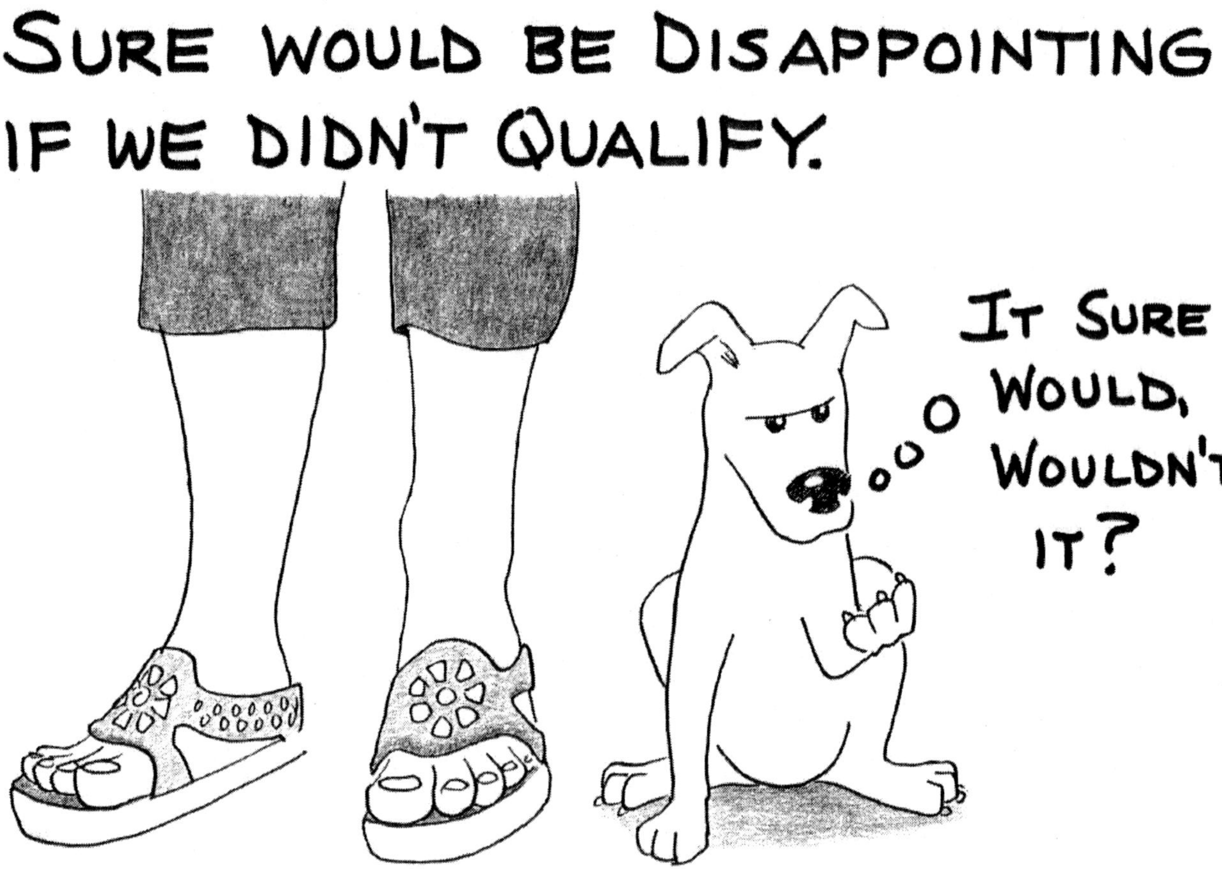
SURE WOULD BE DISAPPOINTING IF WE DIDN'T QUALIFY.
IT SURE WOULD, WOULDN'T IT?

IN ORDER TO EXCEL IN THE SHOW RING THERE MUST EXIST AN UNSPOKEN, ALMOST PSYCHIC, BOND BETWEEN DOG AND HANDLER.

I BET I CAN GET A TREAT OUTTA THIS.

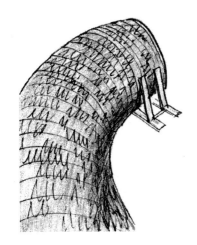

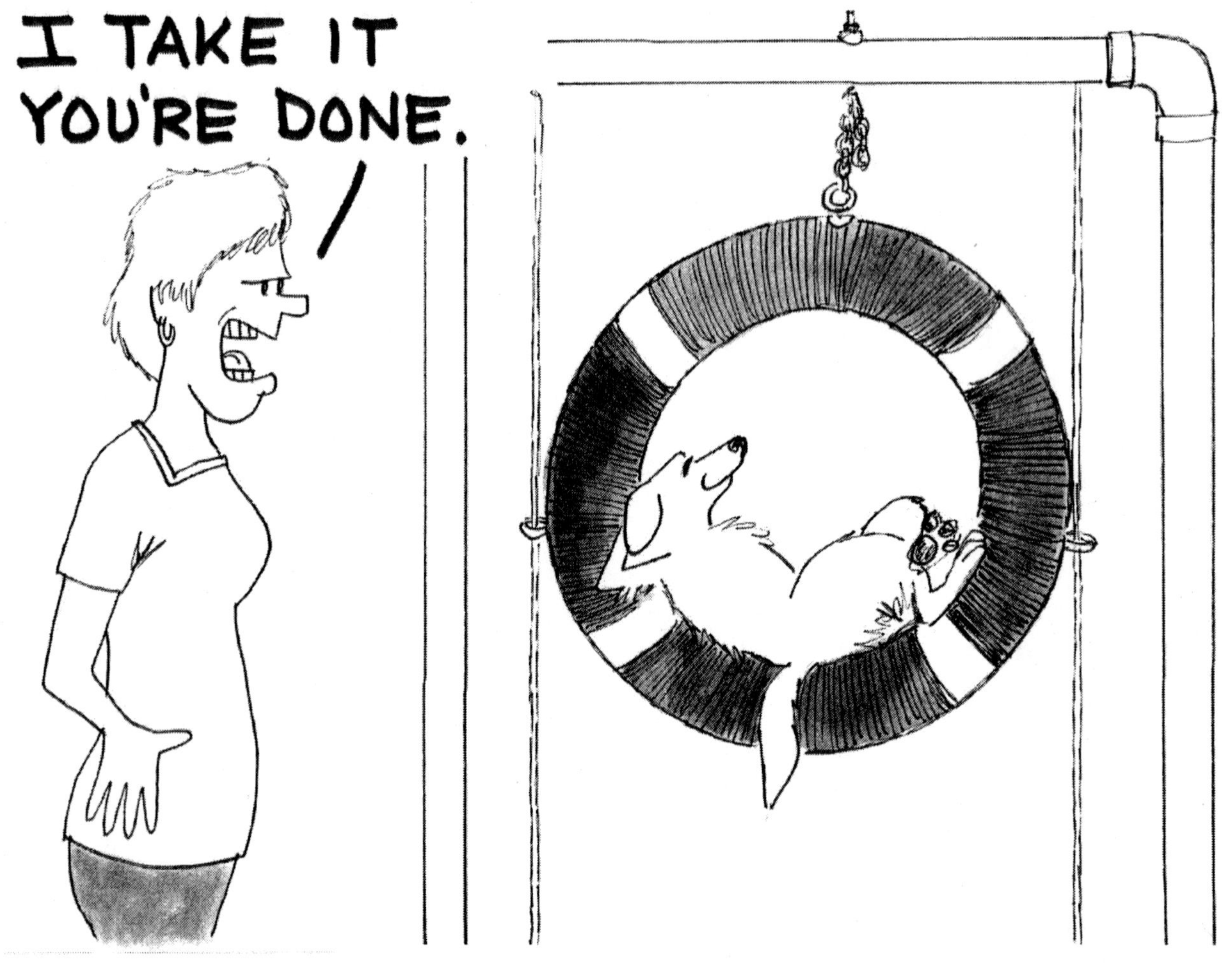
I TAKE IT YOU'RE DONE.

LARRY'S JUDGING CAREER DIDN'T LAST LONG.

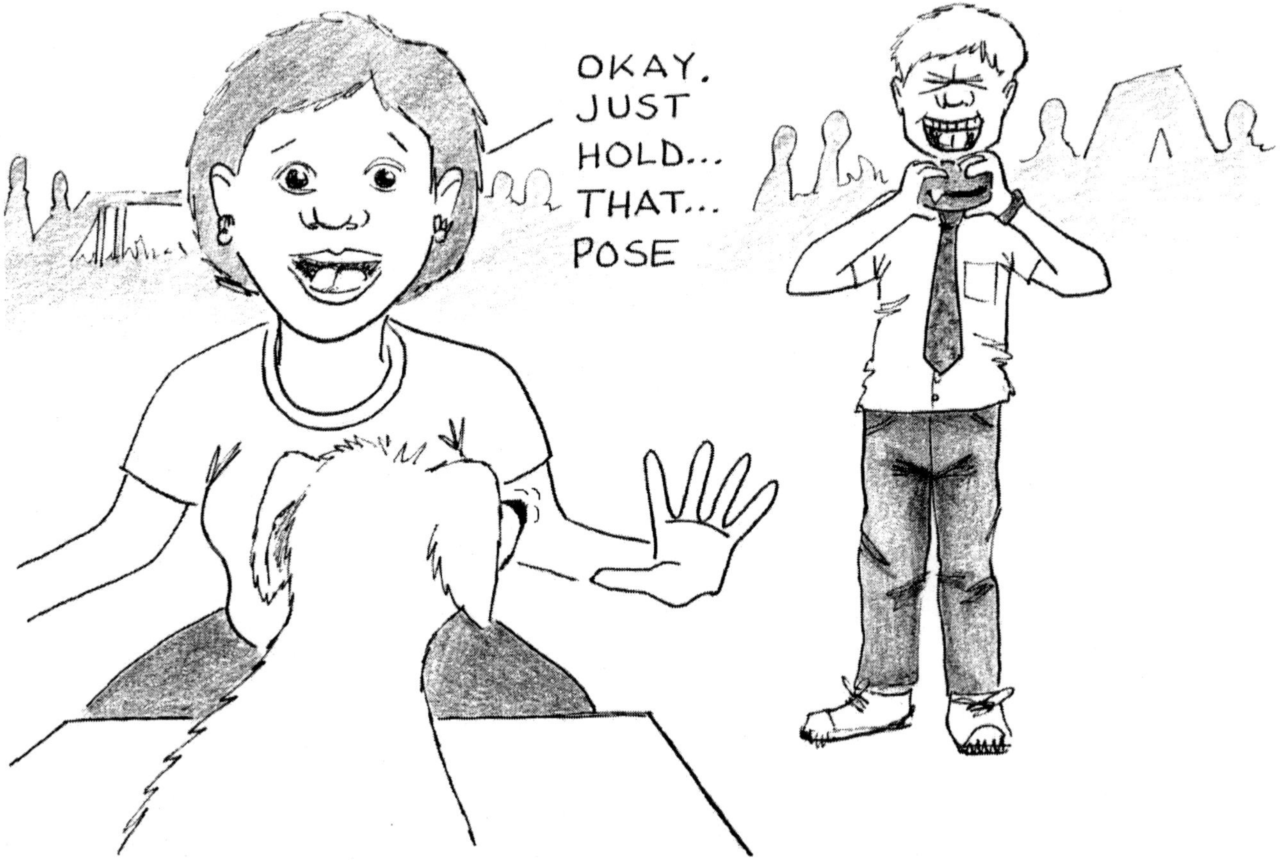
OKAY. JUST HOLD... THAT... POSE

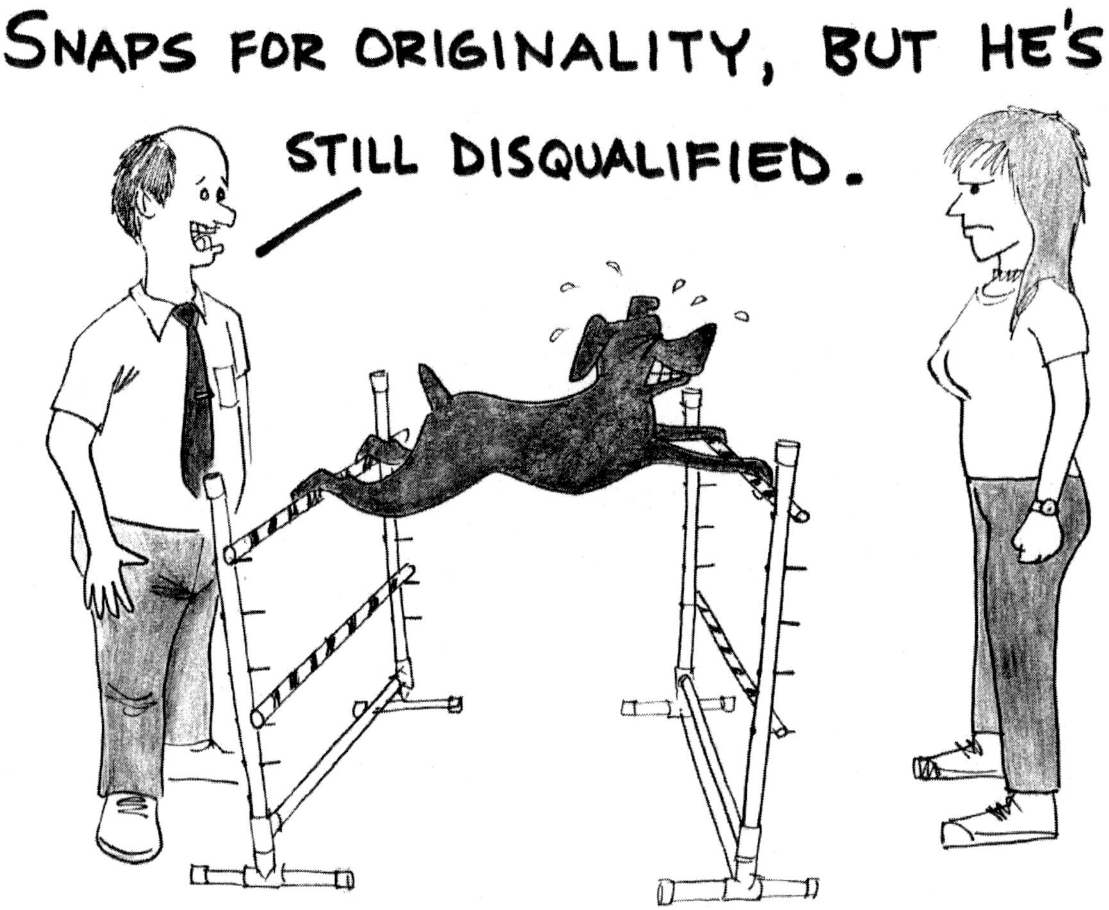
SNAPS FOR ORIGINALITY, BUT HE'S STILL DISQUALIFIED.

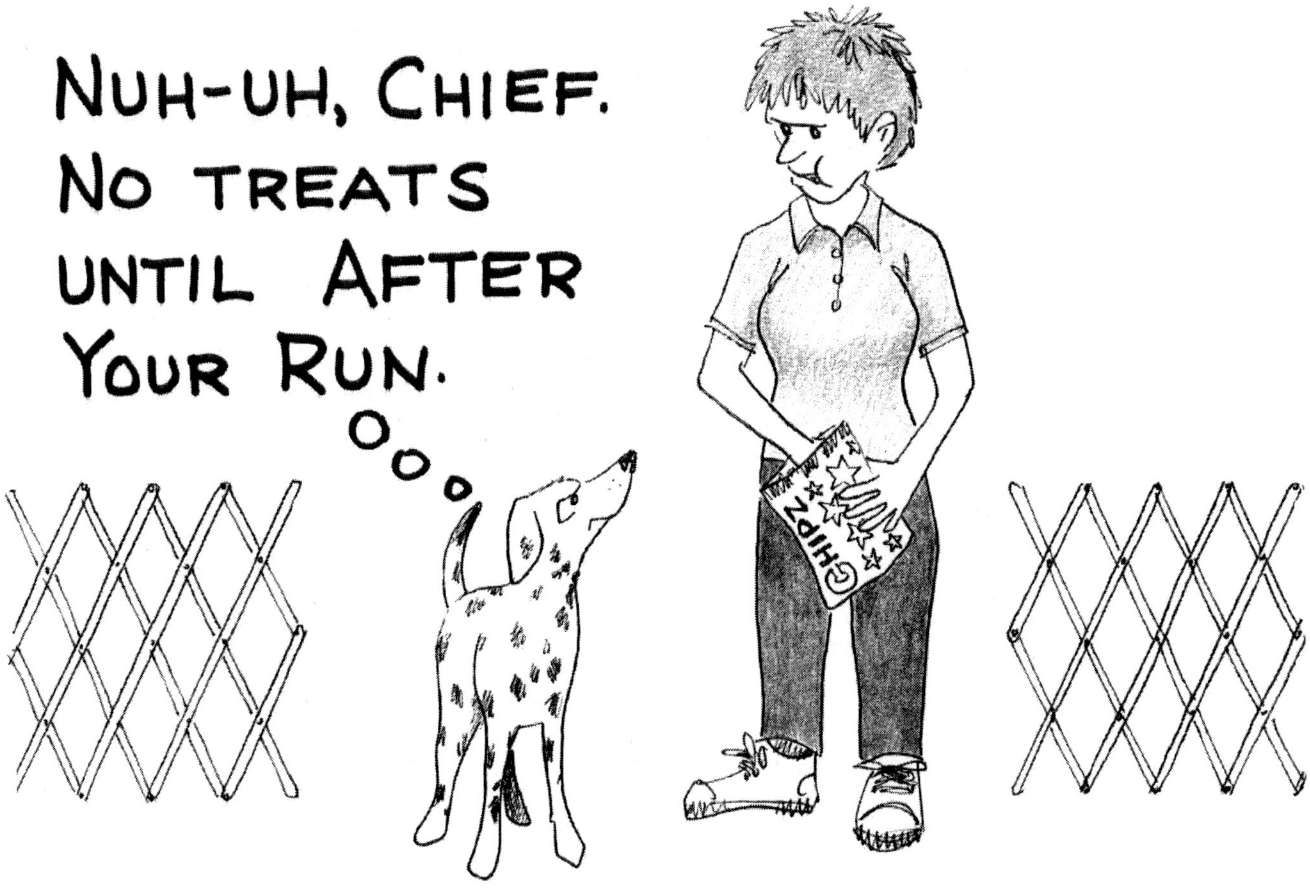
NUH-UH, CHIEF. NO TREATS UNTIL AFTER YOUR RUN.
CHIPZ

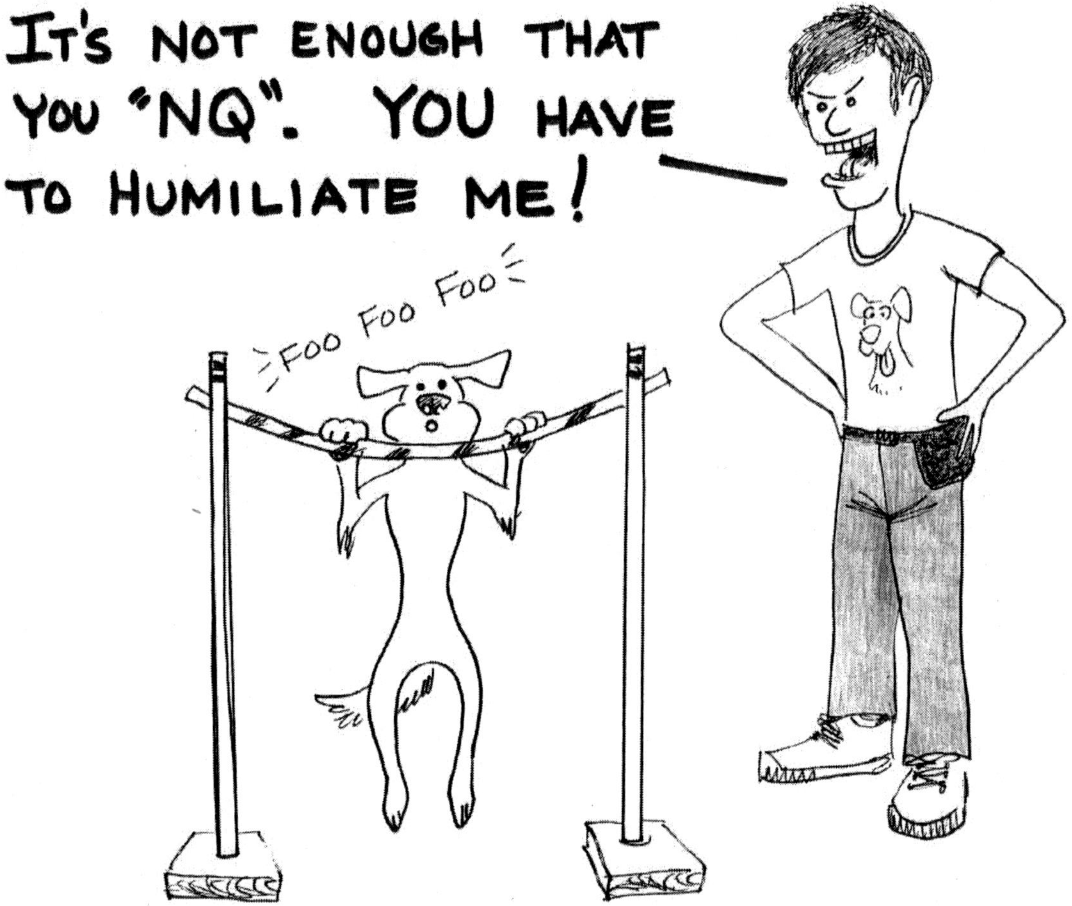
IT'S NOT ENOUGH THAT YOU "NQ". YOU HAVE TO HUMILIATE ME!
FOO FOO FOO

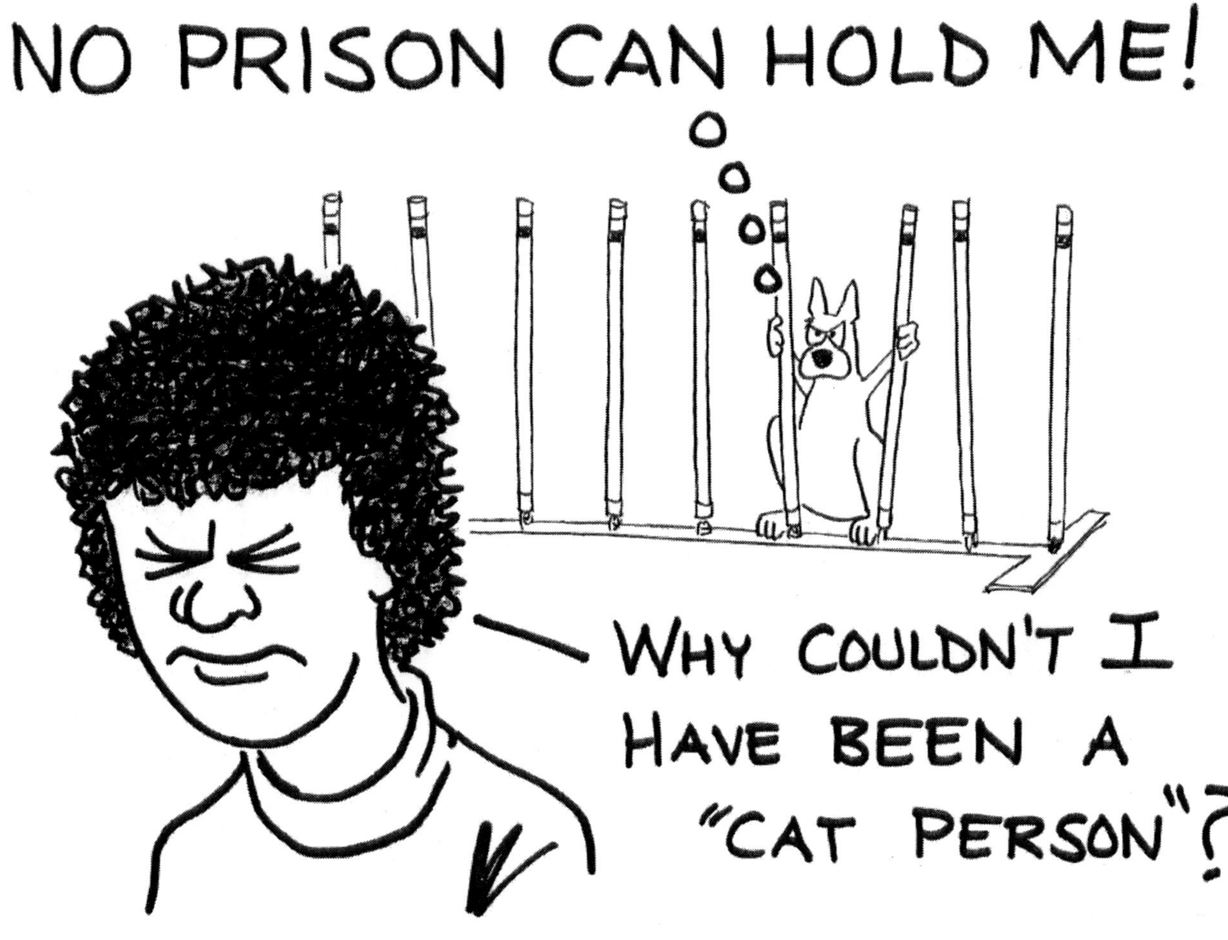
NO PRISON CAN HOLD ME!
WHY COULDN'T I HAVE BEEN A "CAT PERSON"?

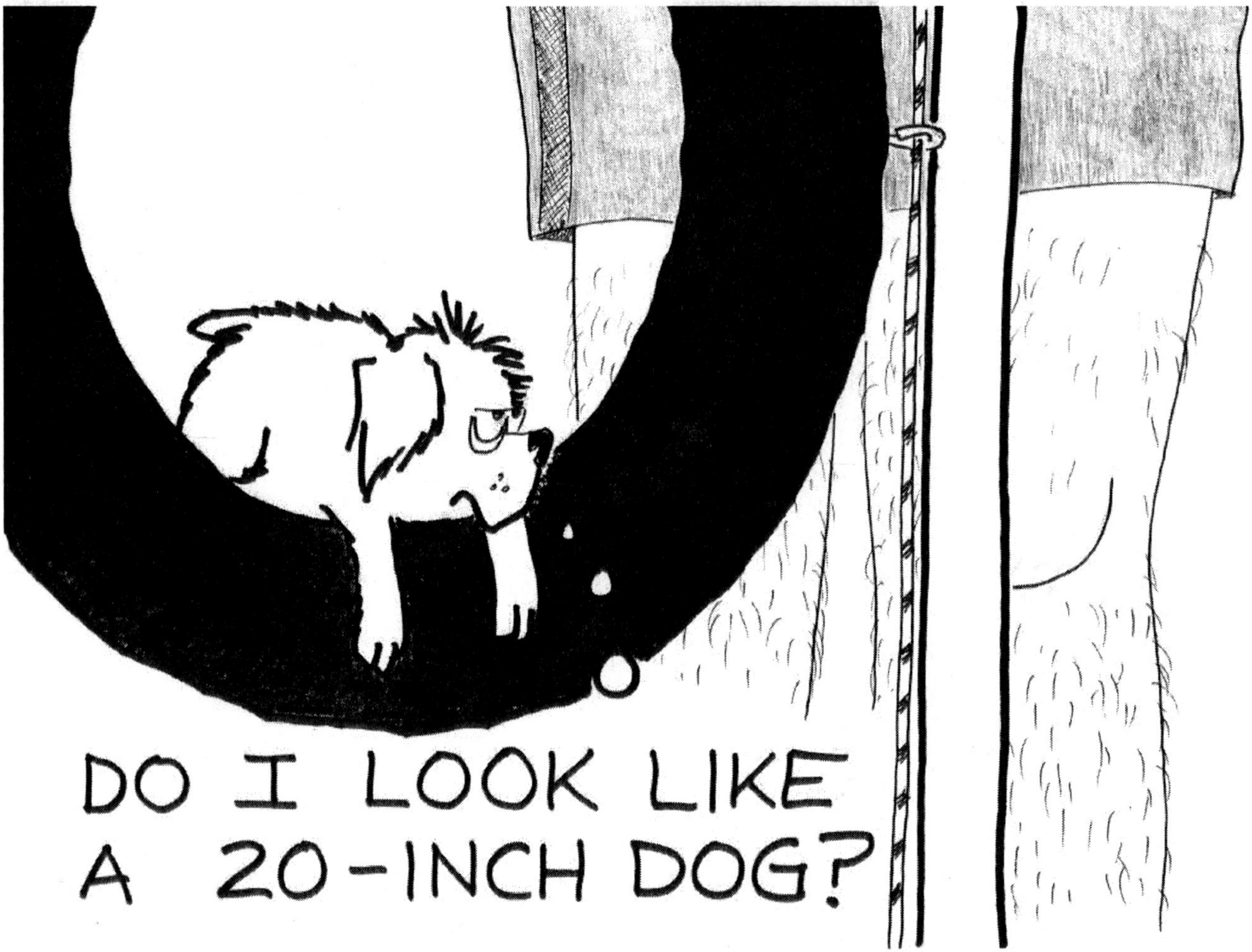
DO I LOOK LIKE
A 20-INCH DOG?

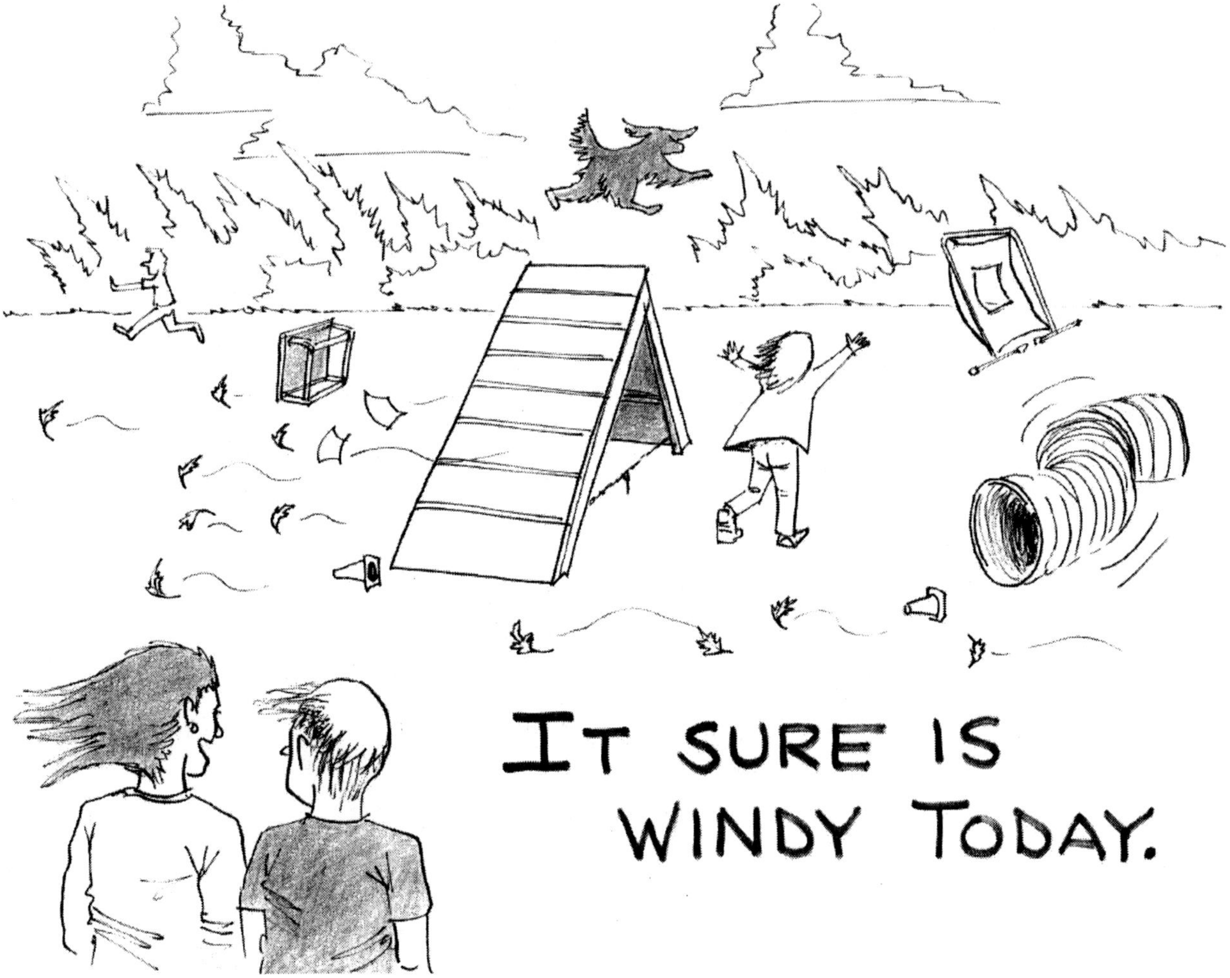
IT SURE IS WINDY TODAY.

WHO ARE YOU
TO JUDGE ME?
JUDGE

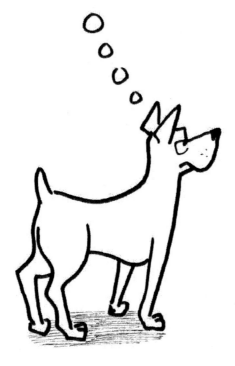

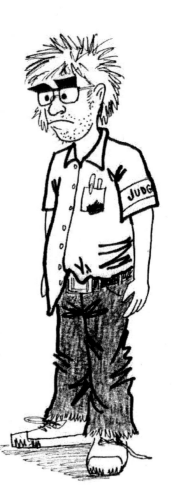

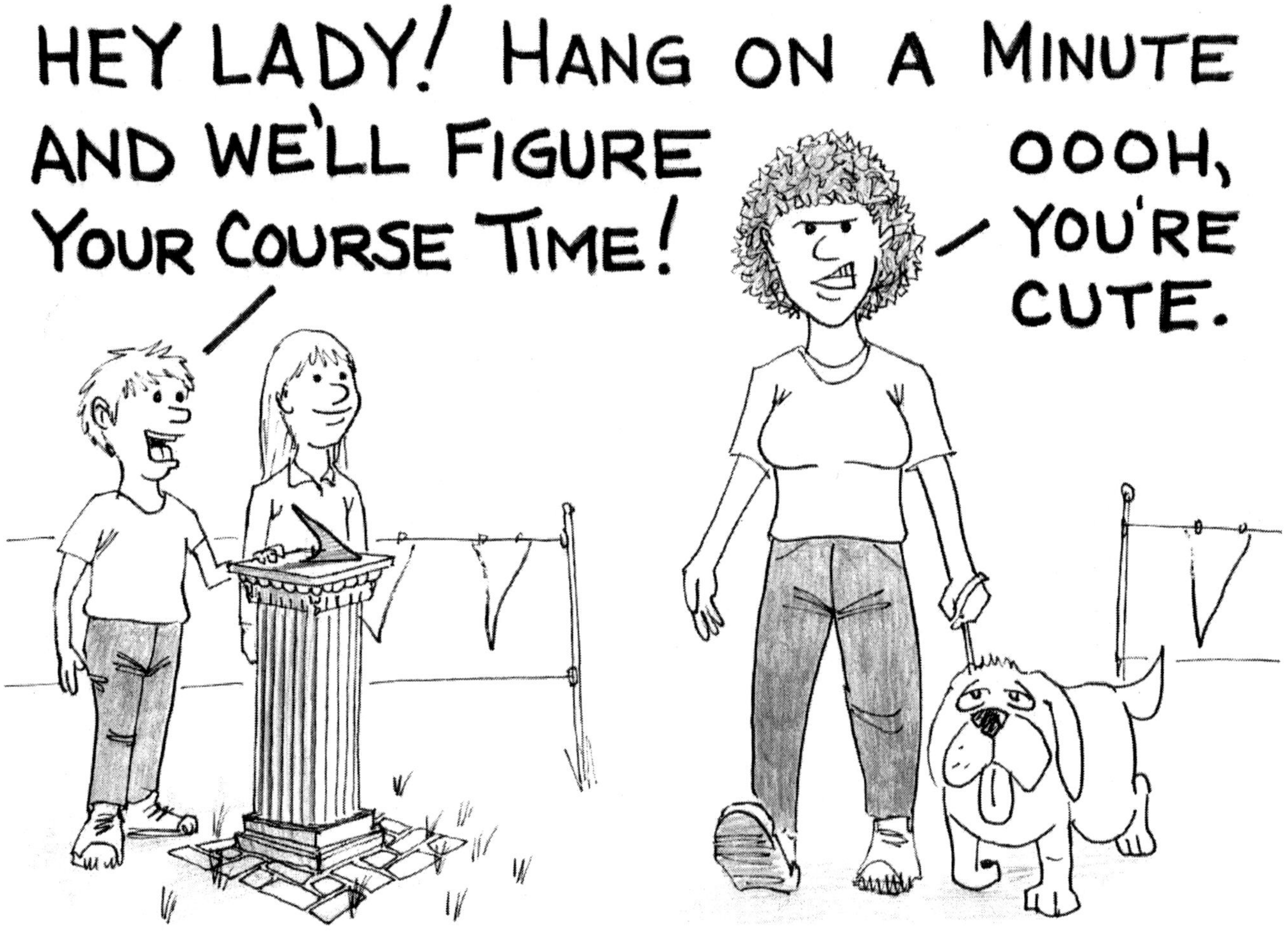
HEY LADY! HANG ON A MINUTE AND WE'LL FIGURE YOUR COURSE TIME!
OOOH, YOU'RE CUTE.

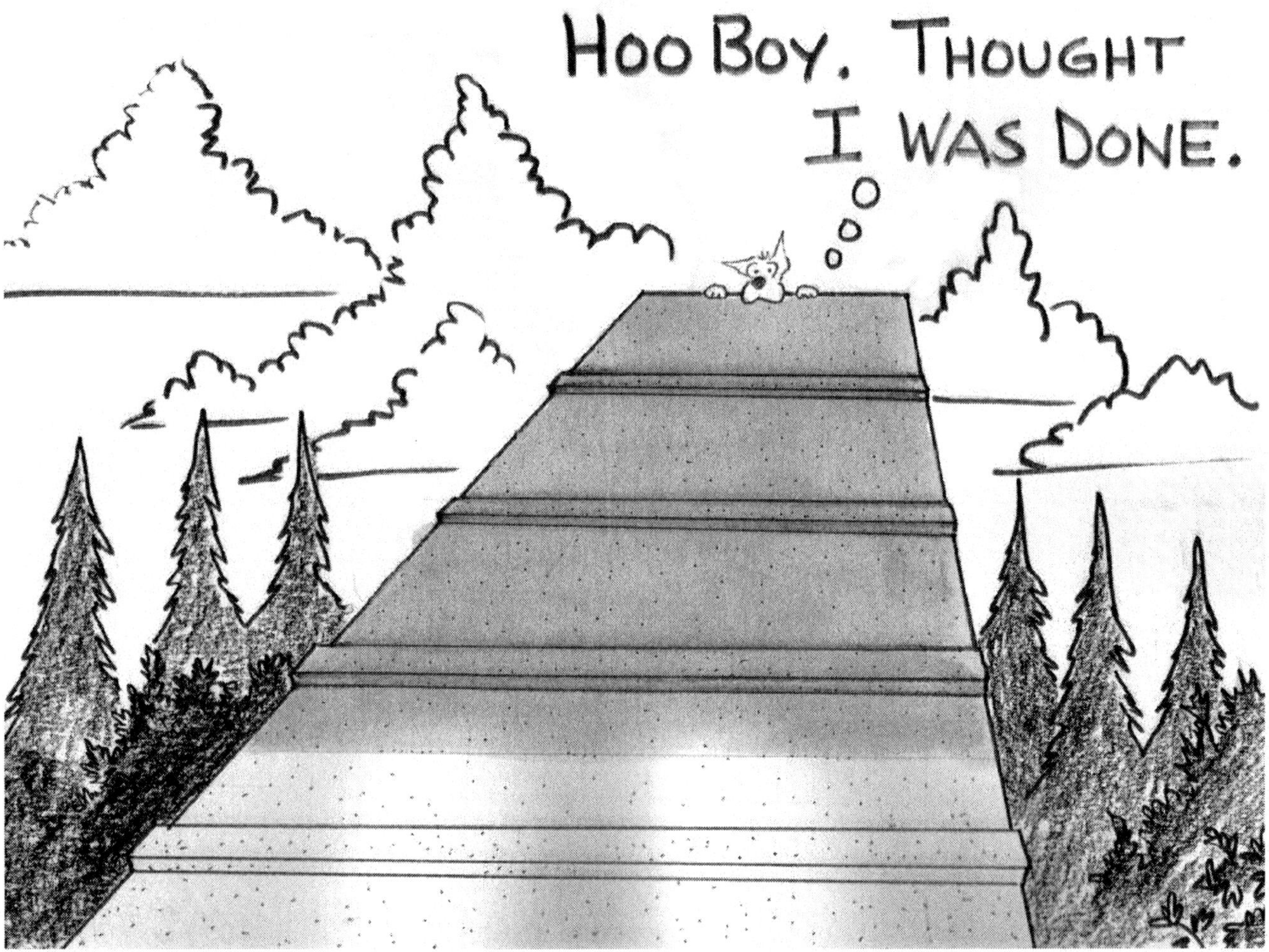
HOO BOY. THOUGHT I WAS DONE.

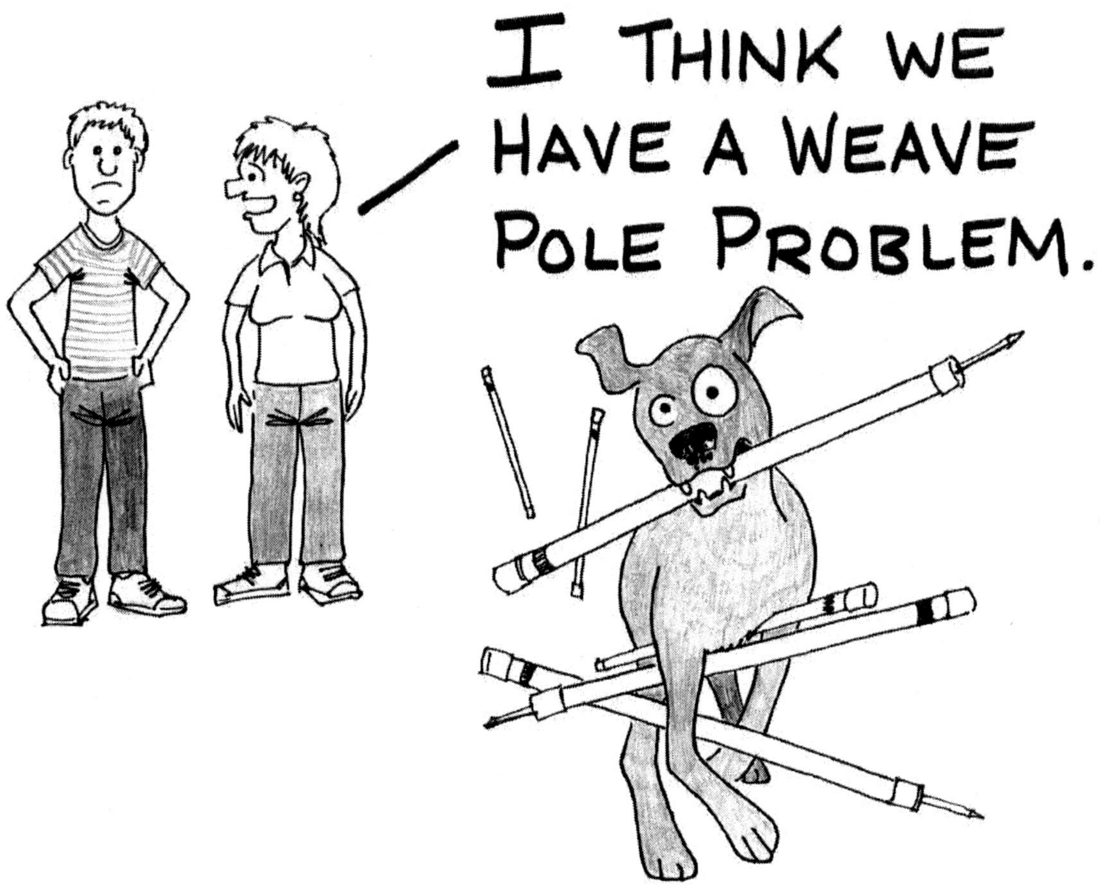
I THINK WE HAVE A WEAVE POLE PROBLEM.

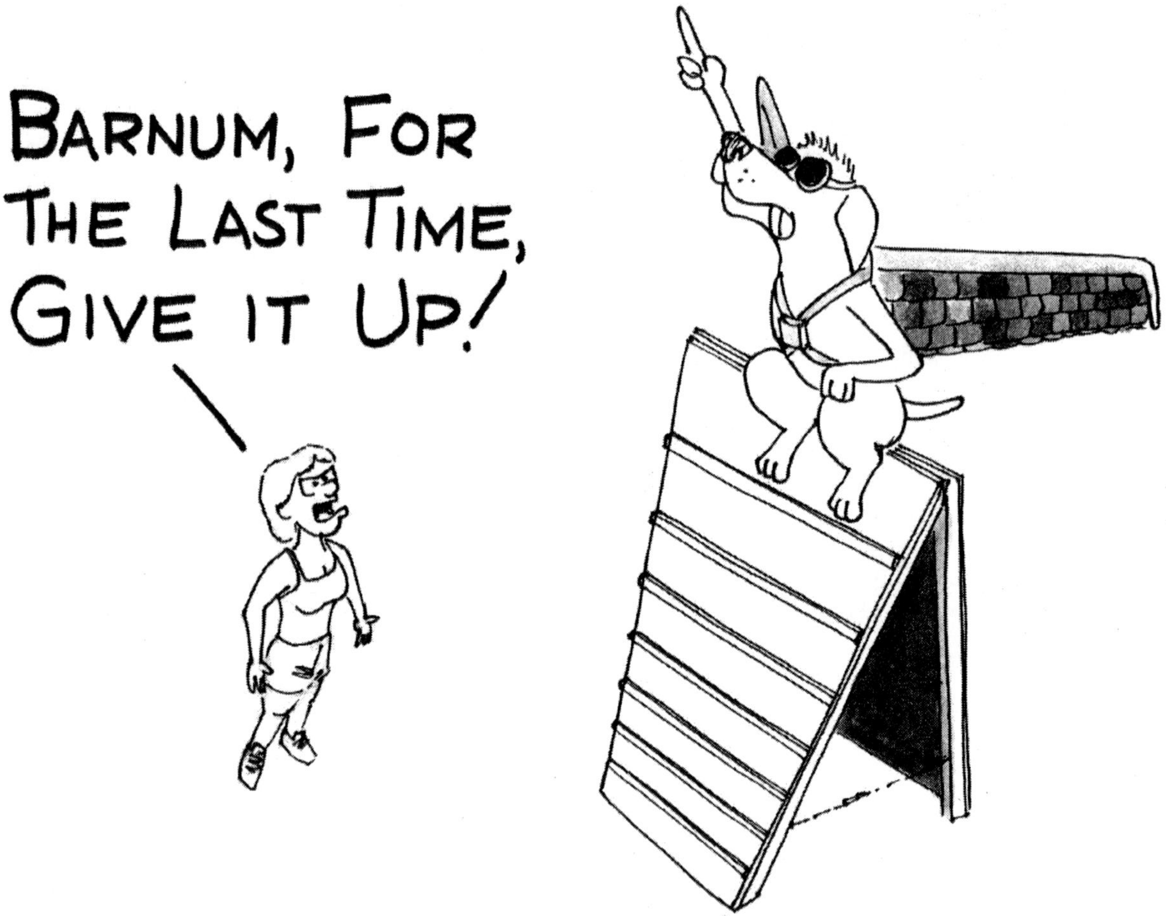
BARNUM, FOR THE LAST TIME, GIVE IT UP!

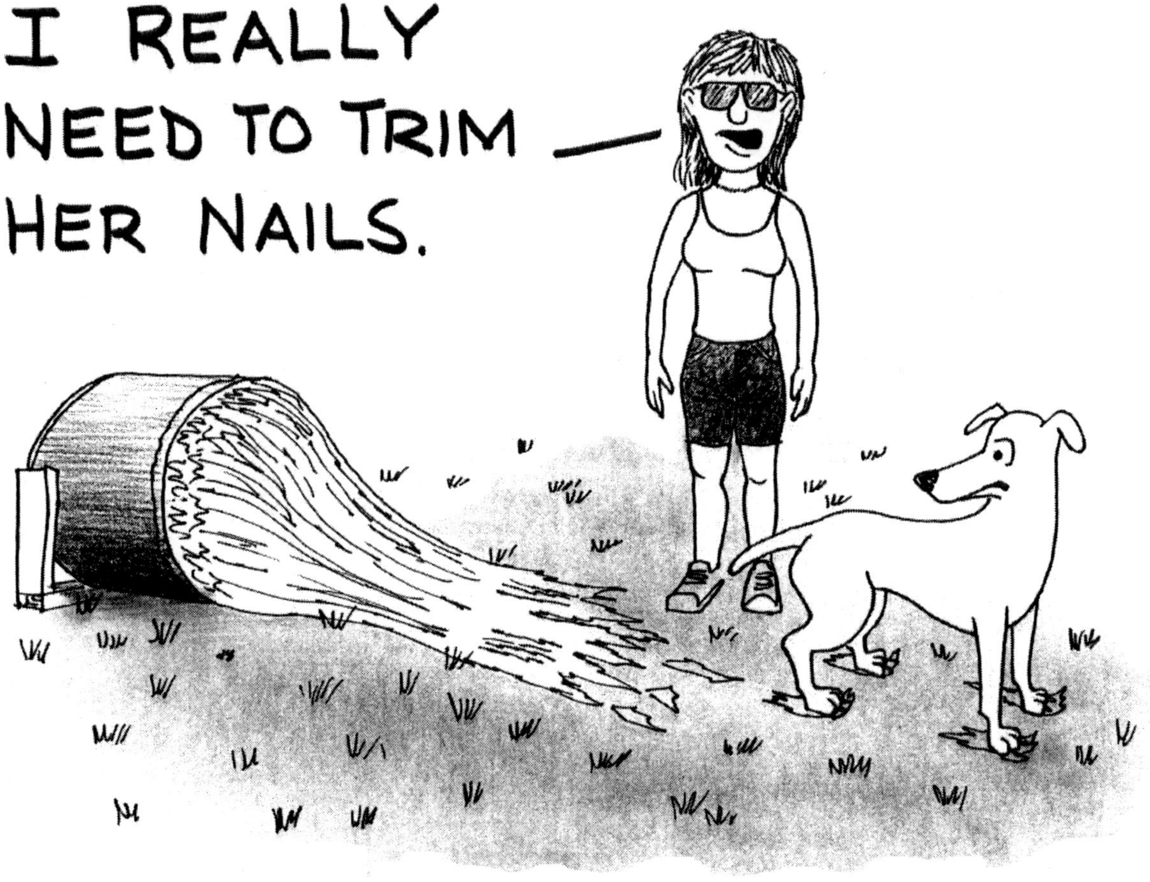
I REALLY NEED TO TRIM HER NAILS.

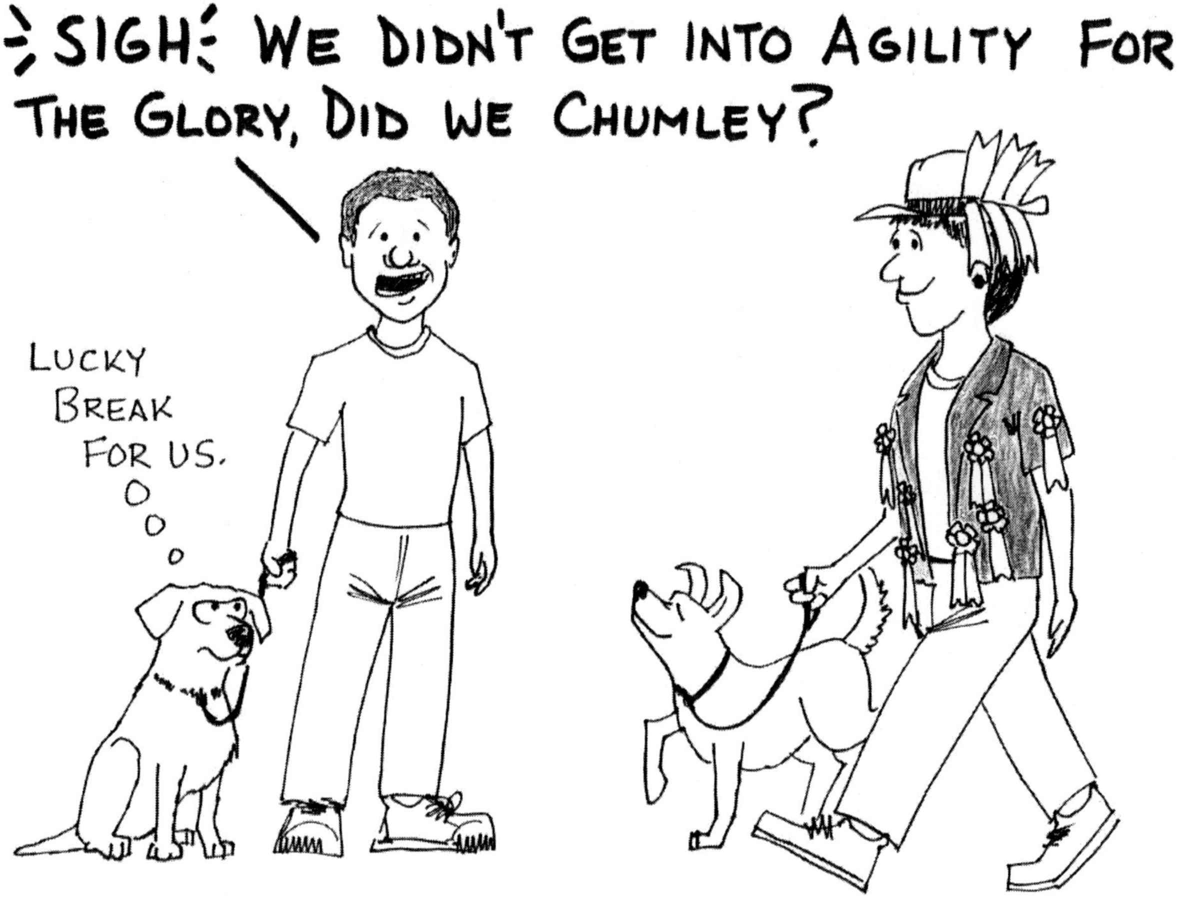
SIGH
WE DIDN'T GET INTO AGILITY FOR THE GLORY, DID WE CHUMLEY?
LUCKY BREAK FOR US.

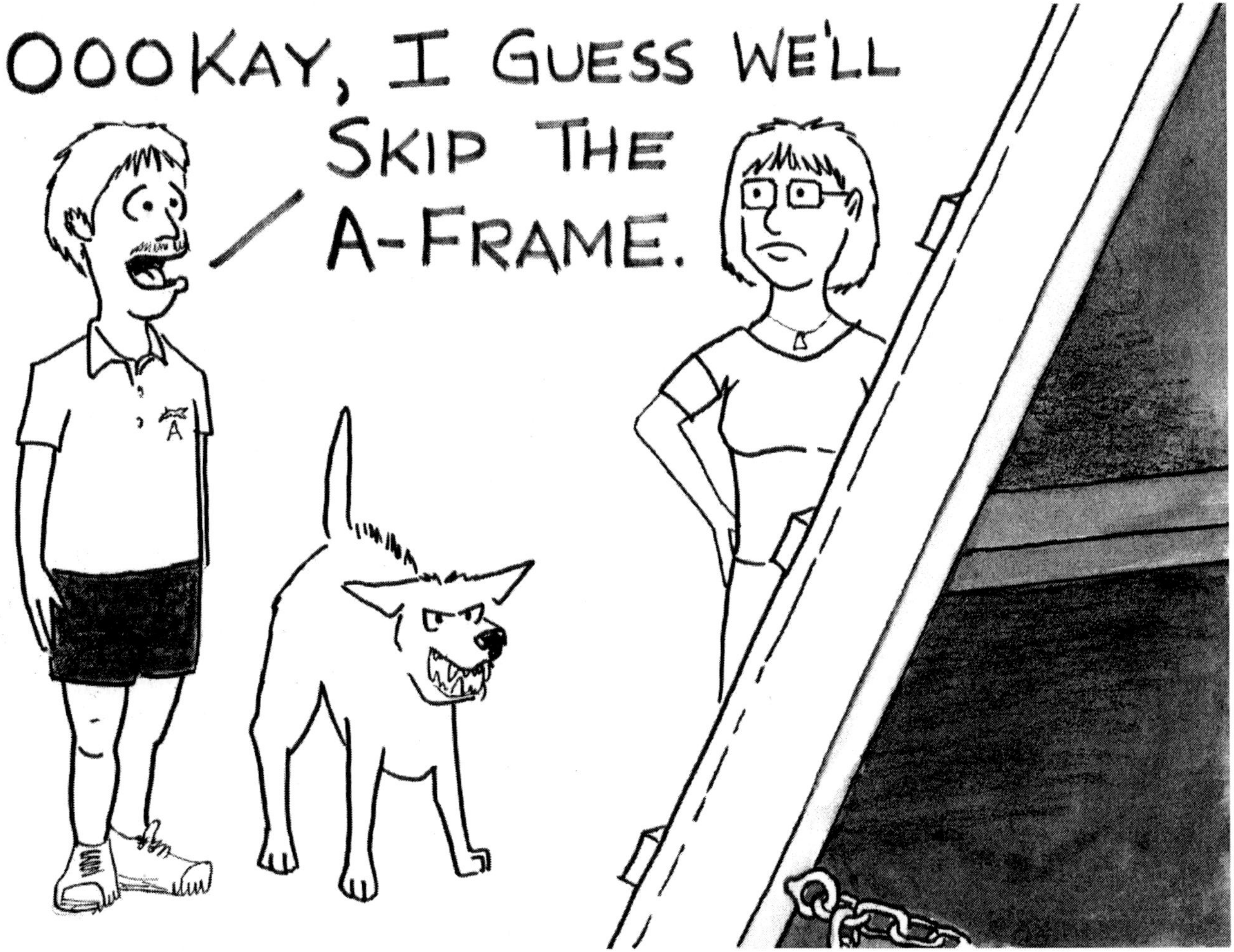
OOOKAY, I GUESS WE'LL SKIP THE A-FRAME.

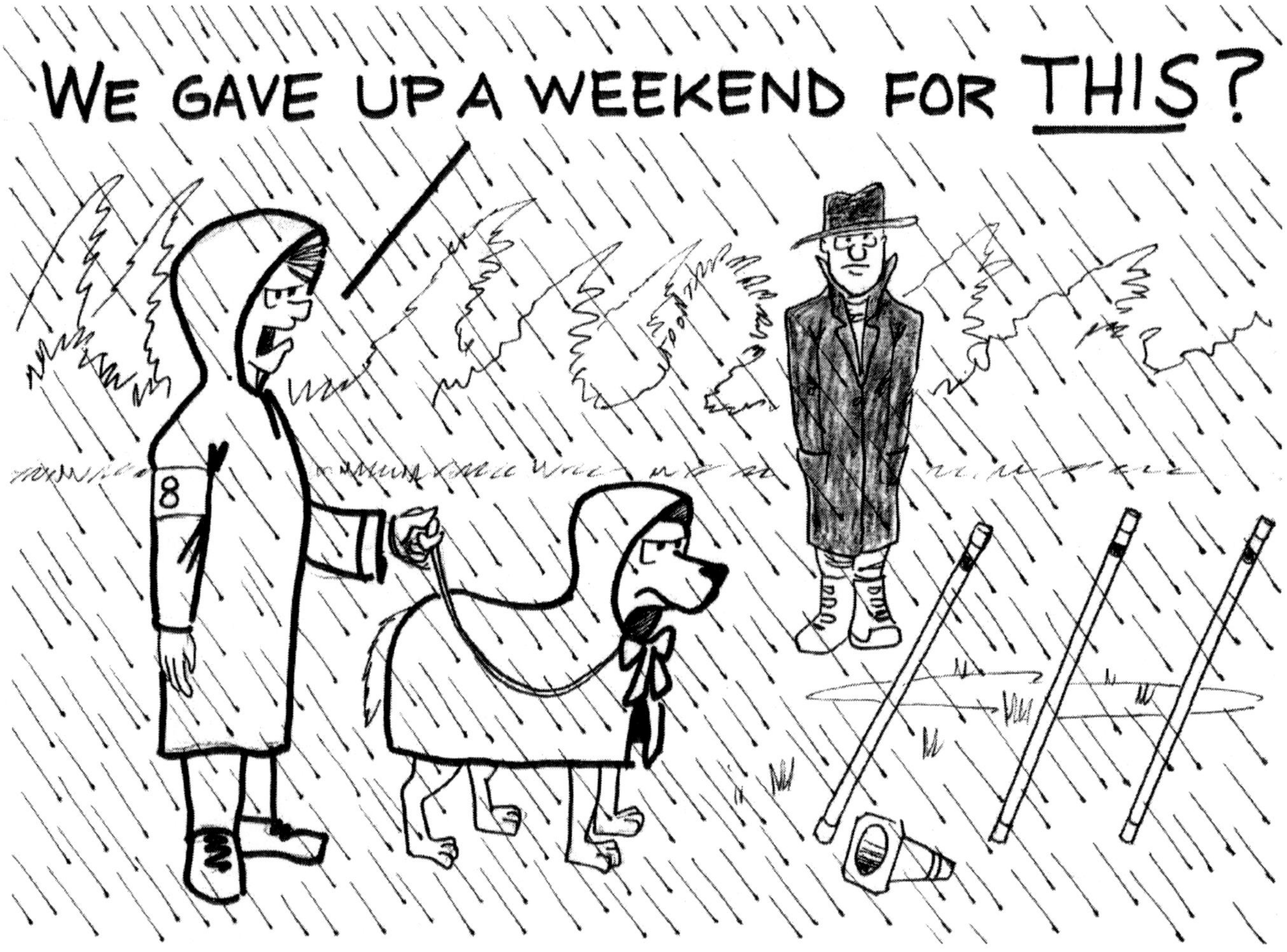
WE GAVE UP A WEEKEND FOR THIS?
8

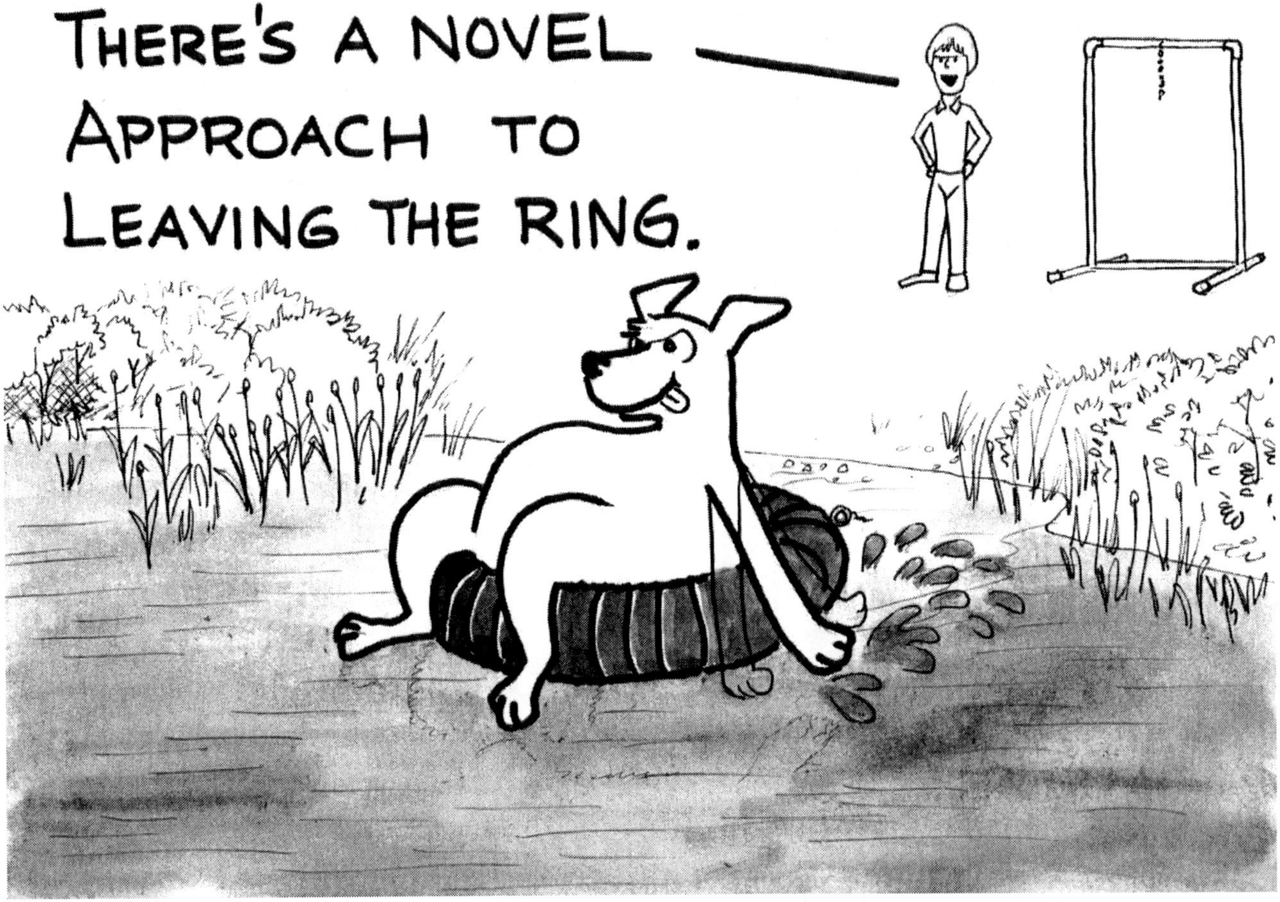
THERE'S A NOVEL APPROACH TO LEAVING THE RING.

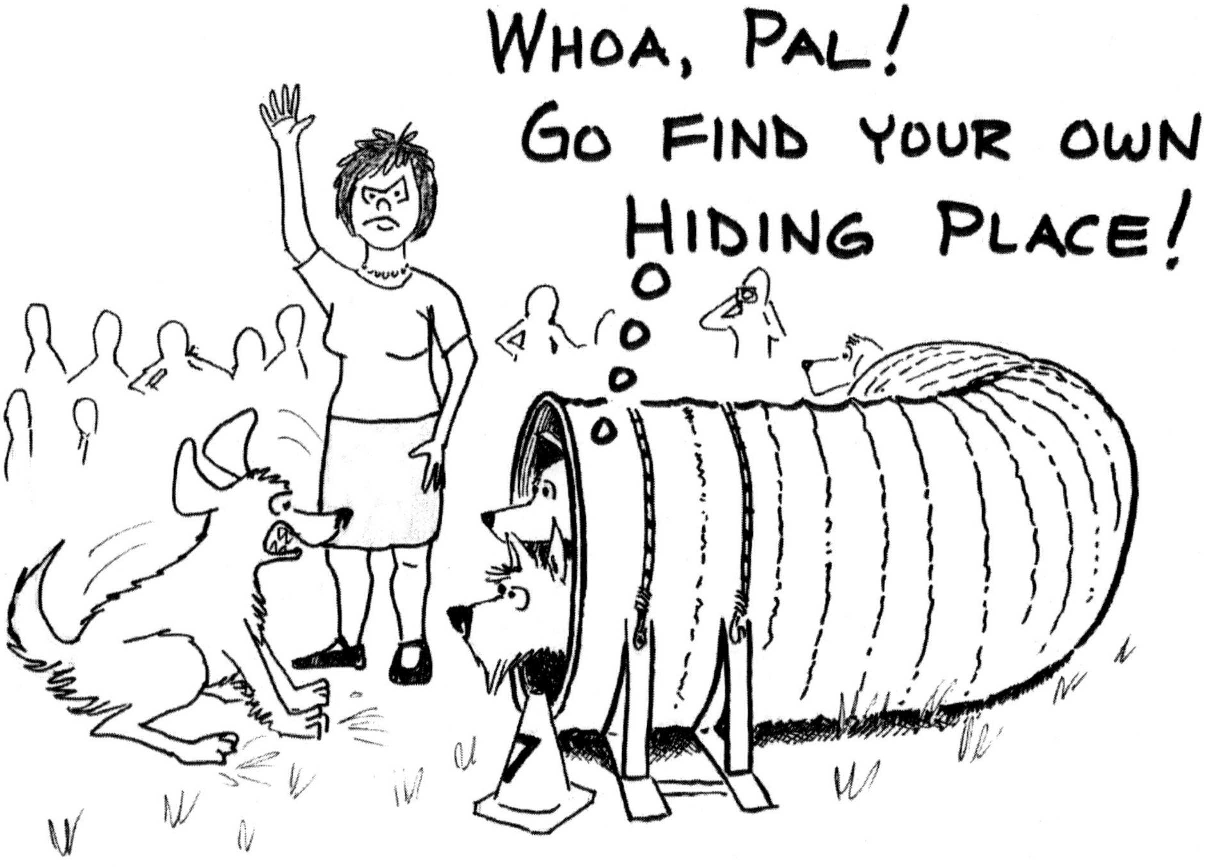
WHOA, PAL!
GO FIND YOUR OWN
HIDING PLACE!
7

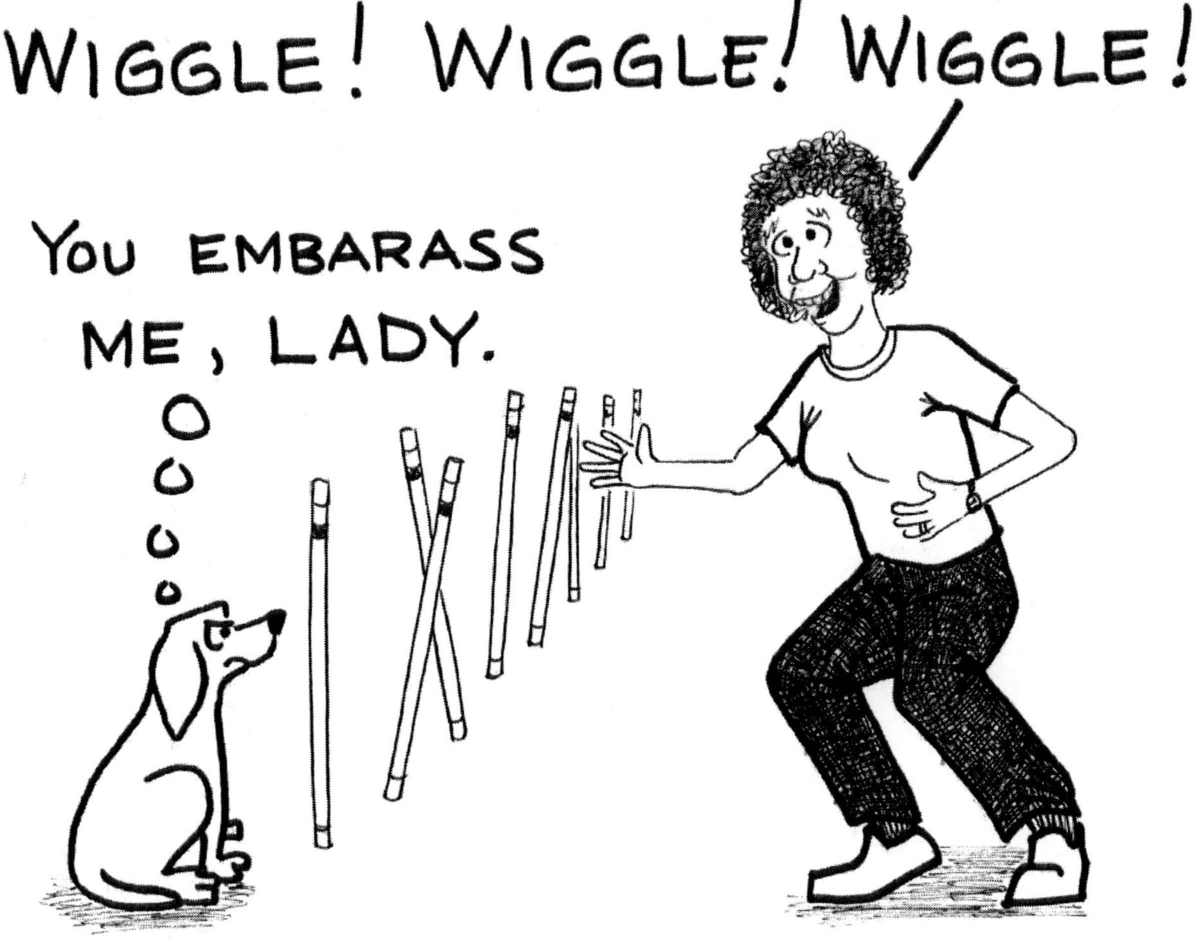
WIGGLE! WIGGLE! WIGGLE!
YOU EMBARASS ME, LADY.

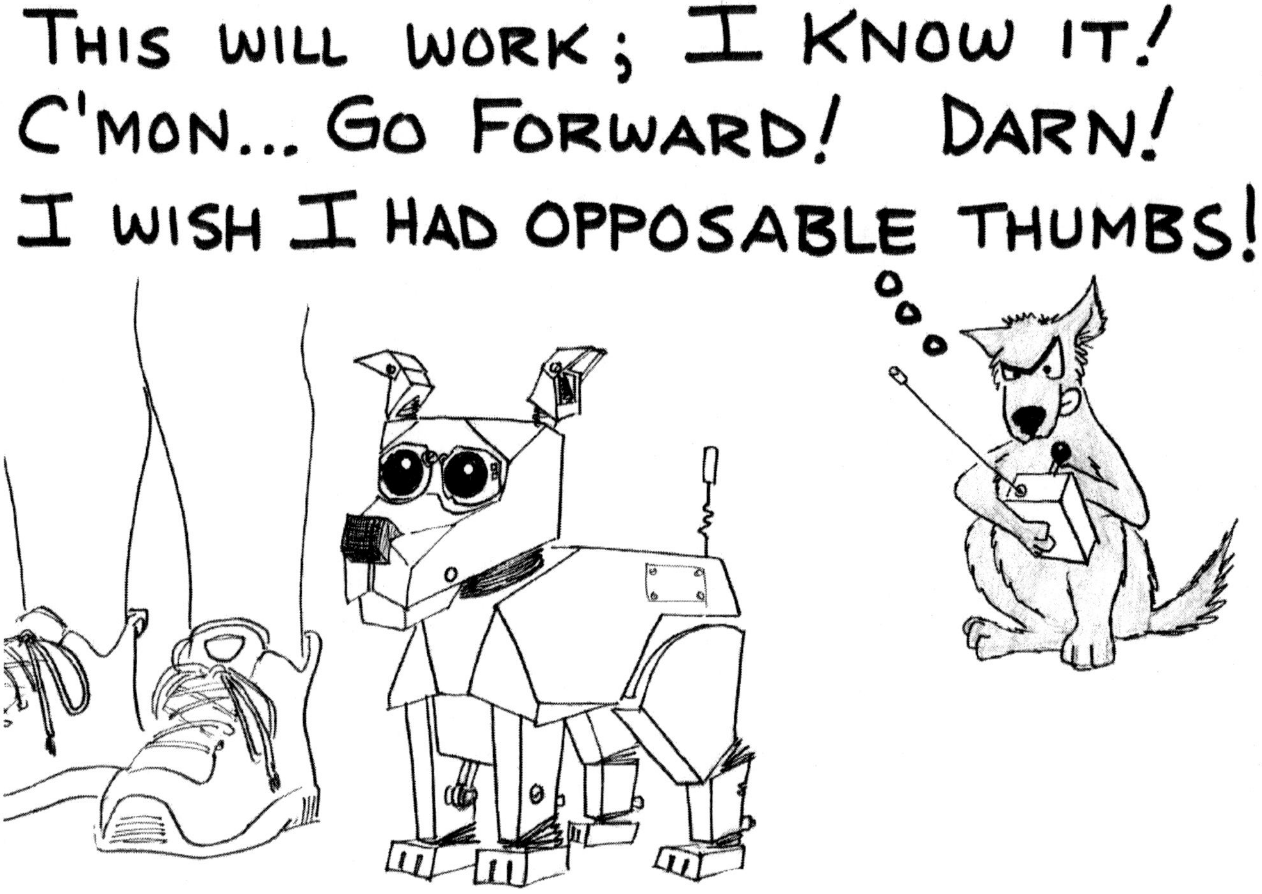
THIS WILL WORK; I KNOW IT!
C'MON... GO FORWARD! DARN!
I WISH I HAD OPPOSABLE THUMBS!

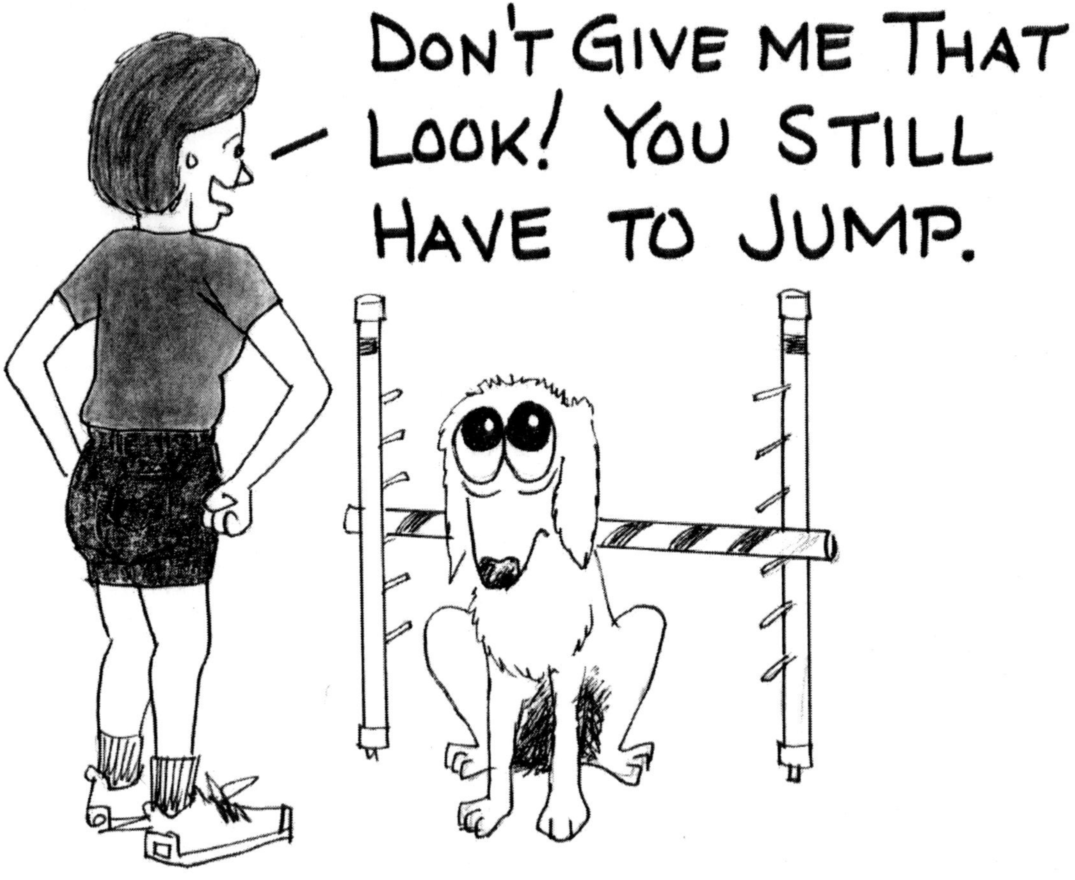
DON'T GIVE ME THAT LOOK! YOU STILL HAVE TO JUMP.

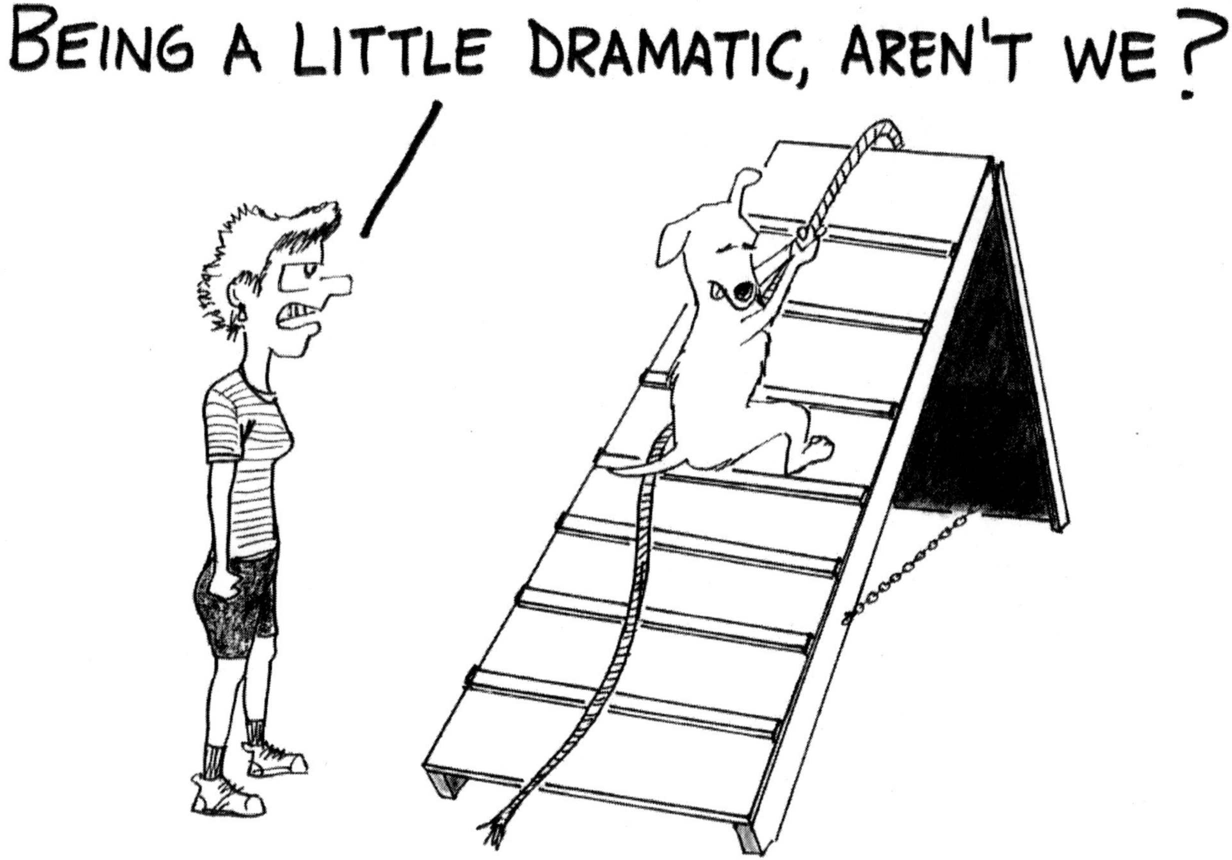
BEING A LITTLE DRAMATIC, AREN'T WE?

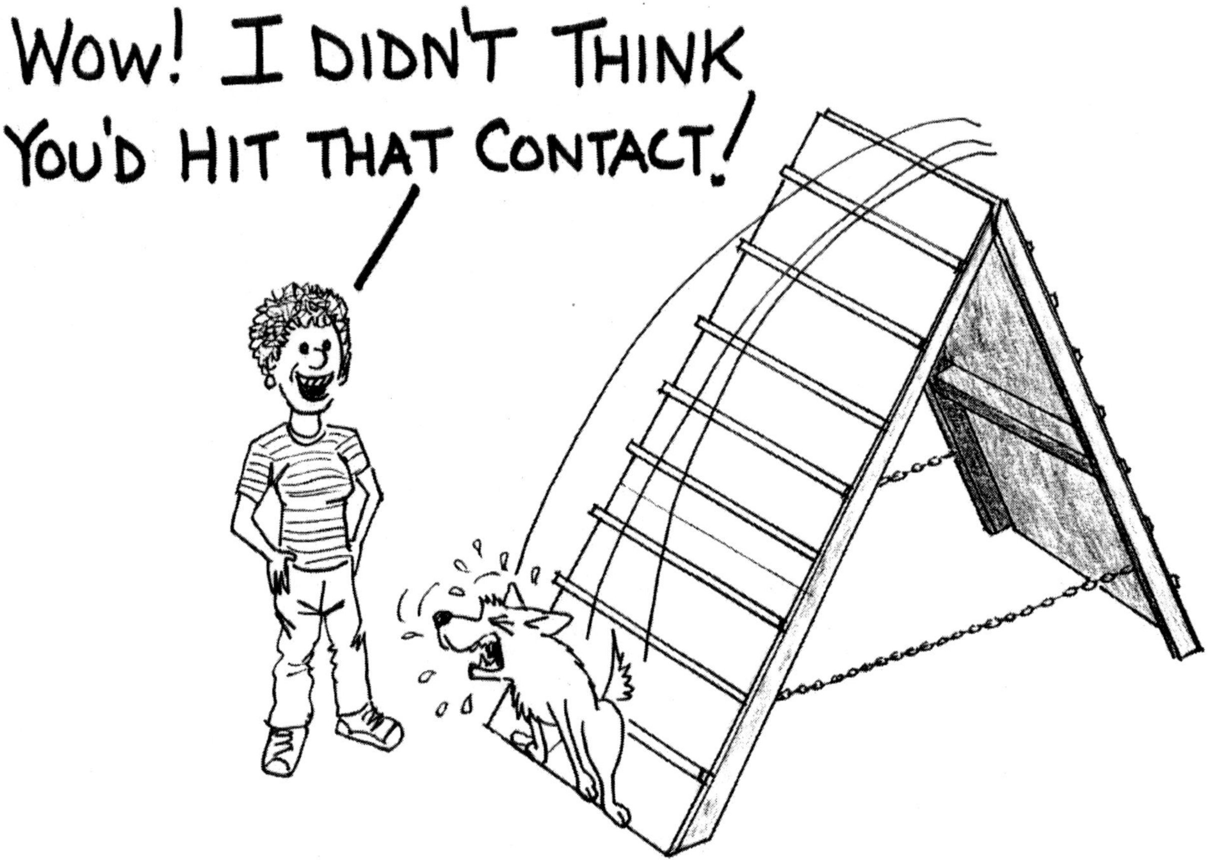
WOW! I DIDN'T THINK YOU'D HIT THAT CONTACT!

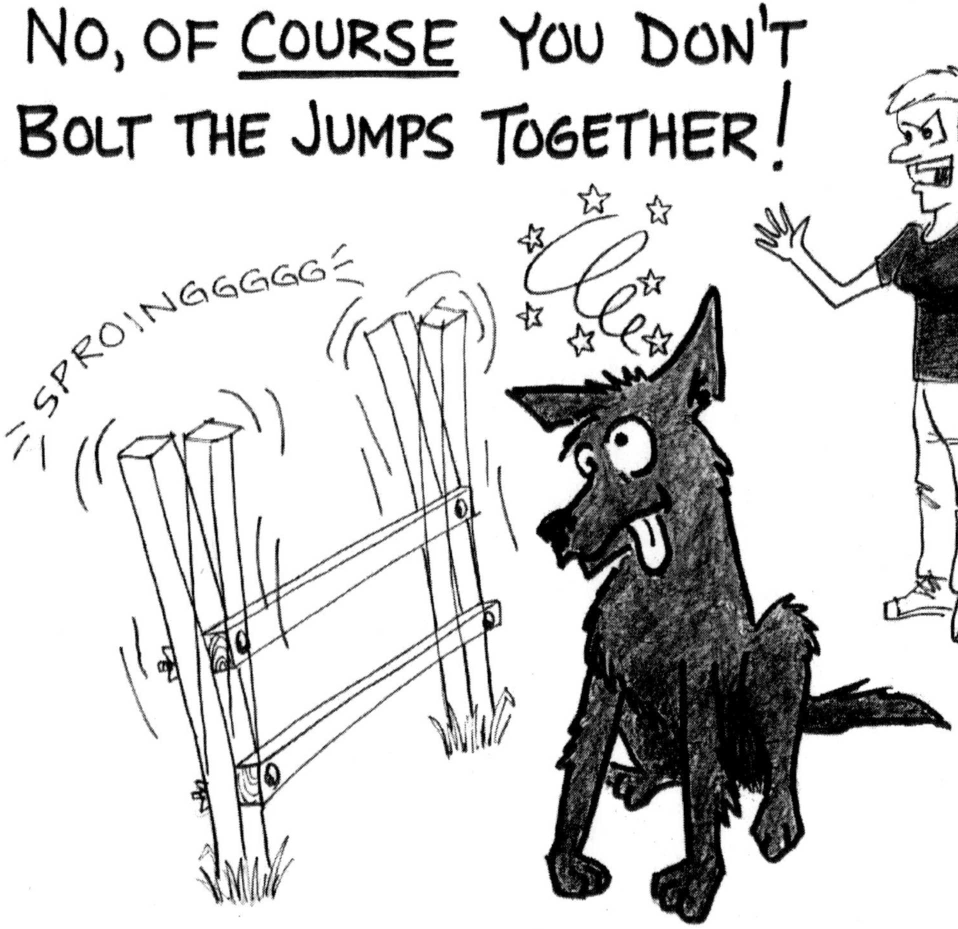
NO, OF COURSE YOU DON'T
BOLT THE JUMPS TOGETHER!
SPROINGGGGGG

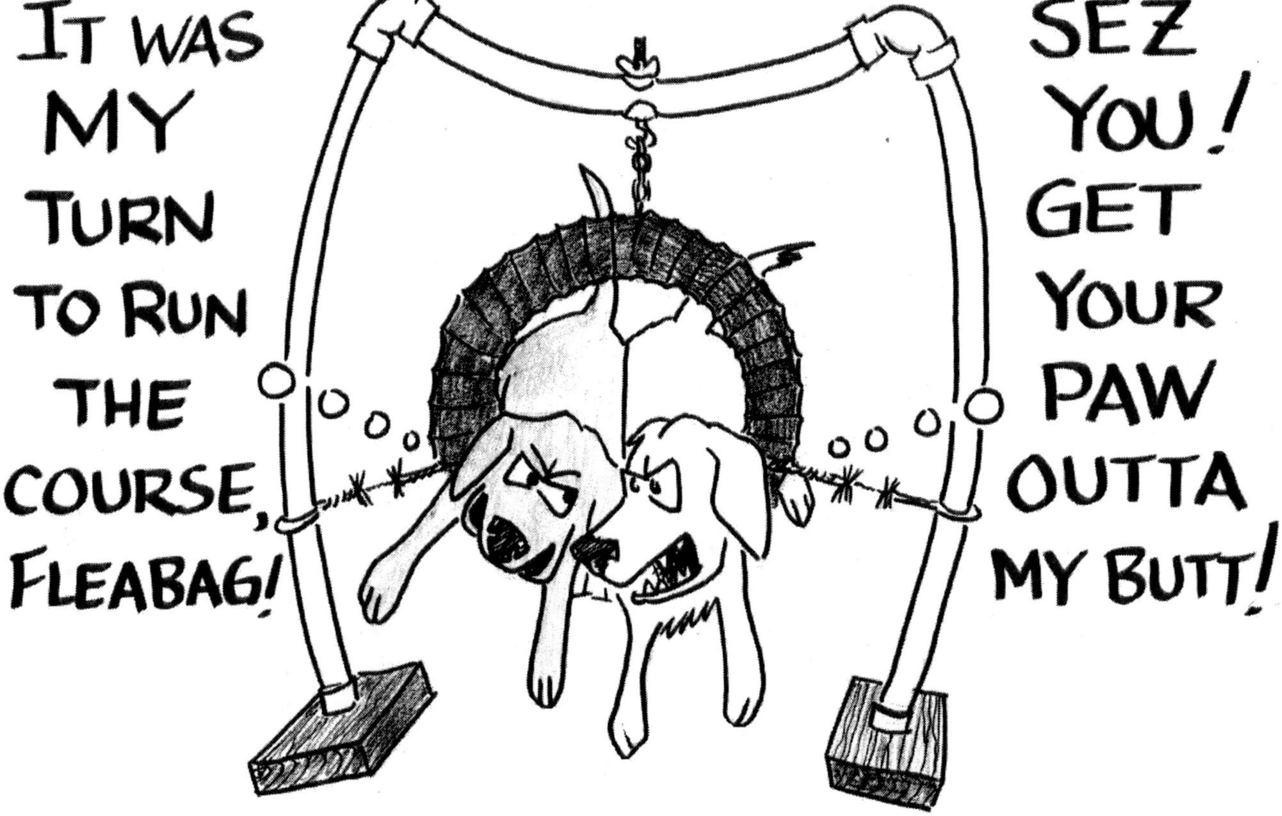
IT WAS MY TURN TO RUN THE COURSE, FLEABAG!
SEZ YOU! GET YOUR PAW OUTTA MY BUTT!

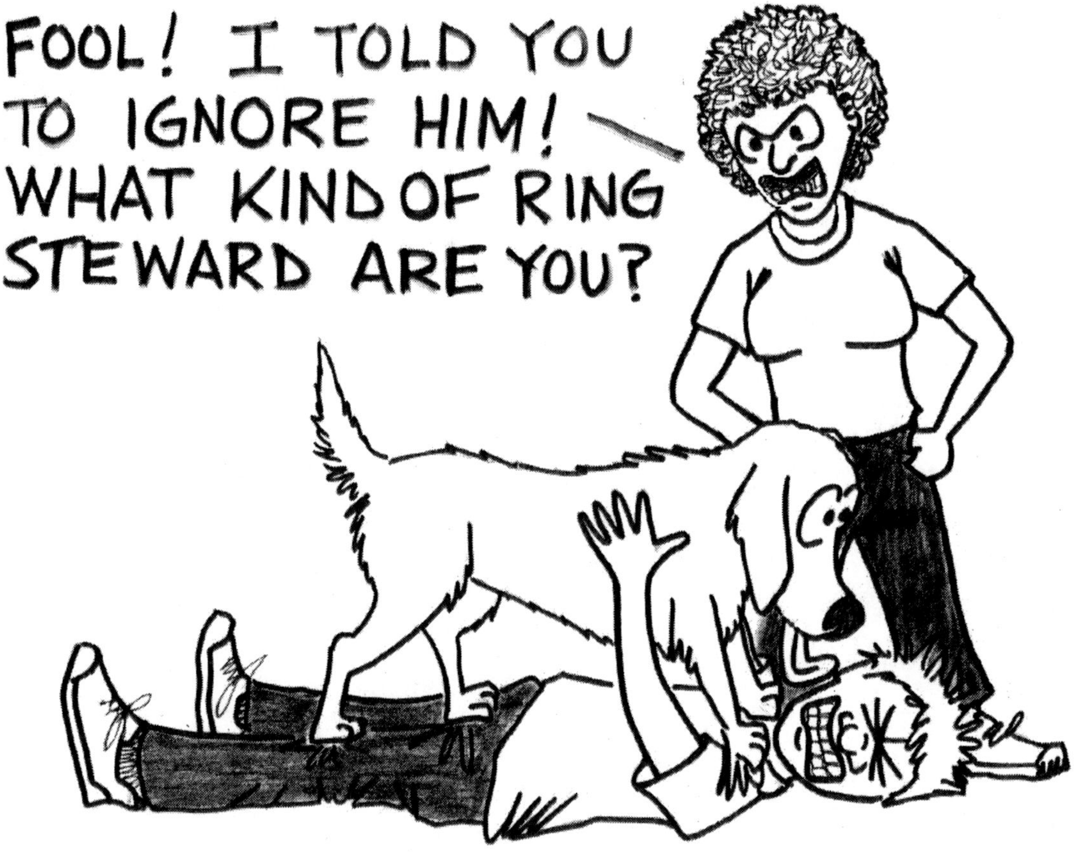
FOOL! I TOLD YOU TO IGNORE HIM! WHAT KIND OF RING STEWARD ARE YOU?

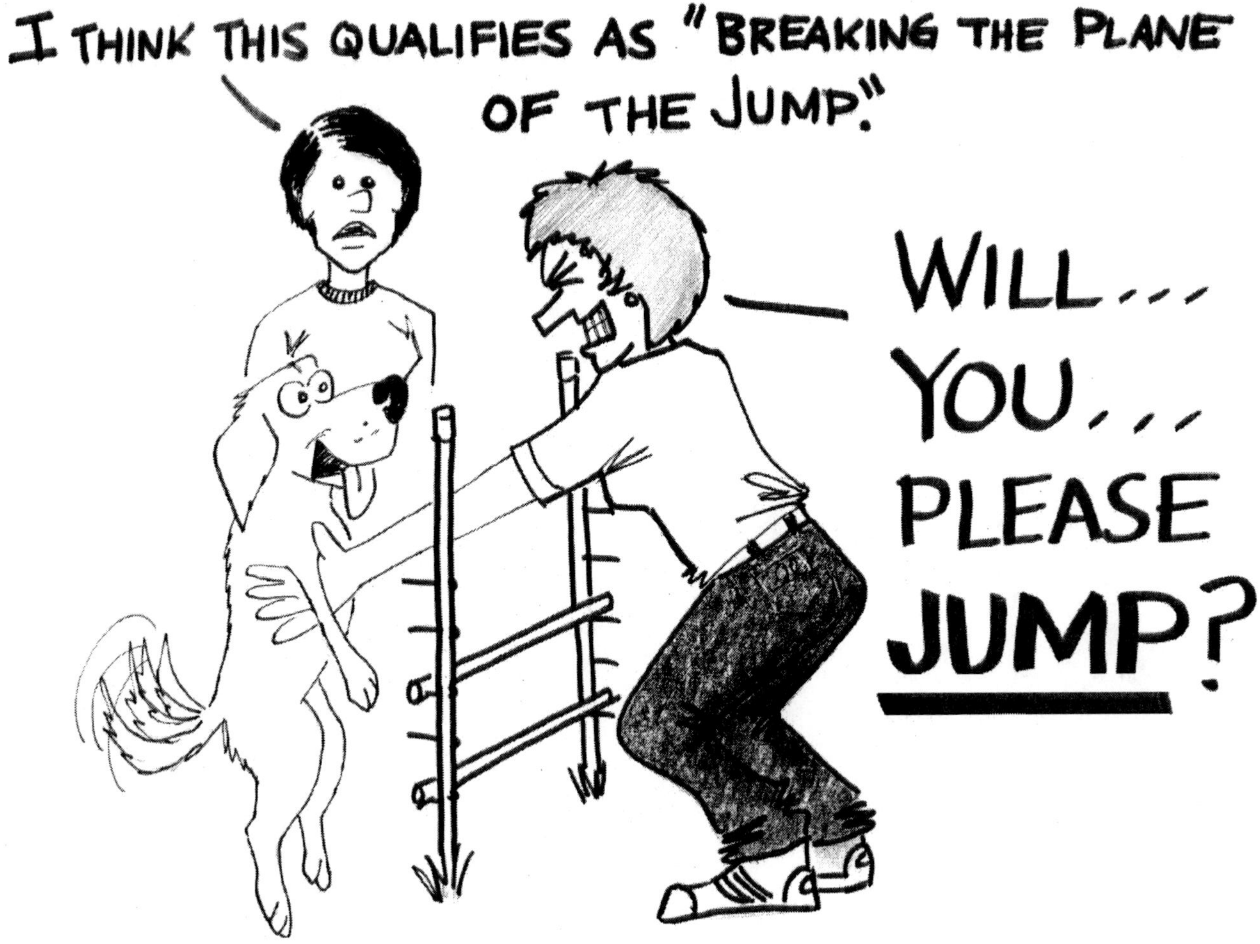
I THINK THIS QUALIFIES AS "BREAKING THE PLANE OF THE JUMP."
WILL... YOU... PLEASE JUMP?

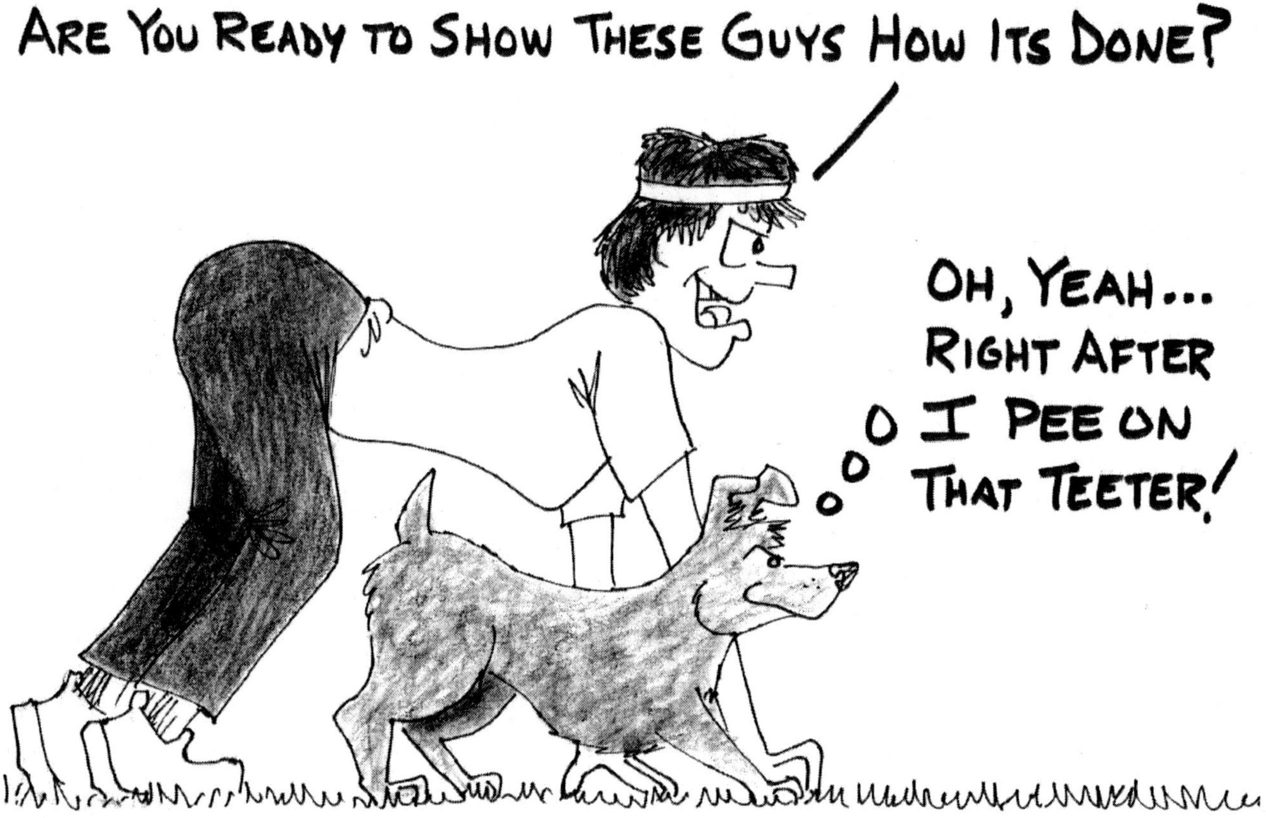
ARE YOU READY TO SHOW THESE GUYS HOW ITS DONE?
OH, YEAH... RIGHT AFTER I PEE ON THAT TEETER!

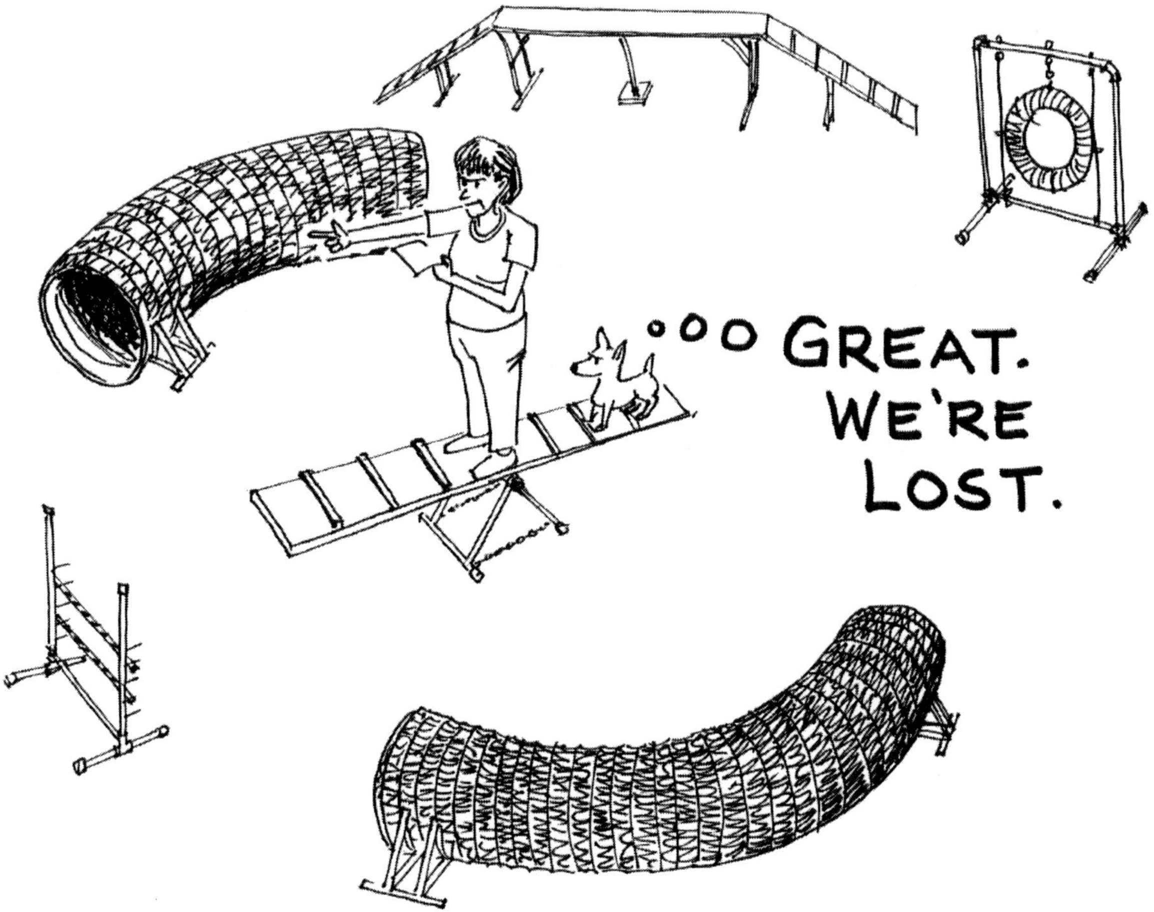
GREAT.
WE'RE
LOST.

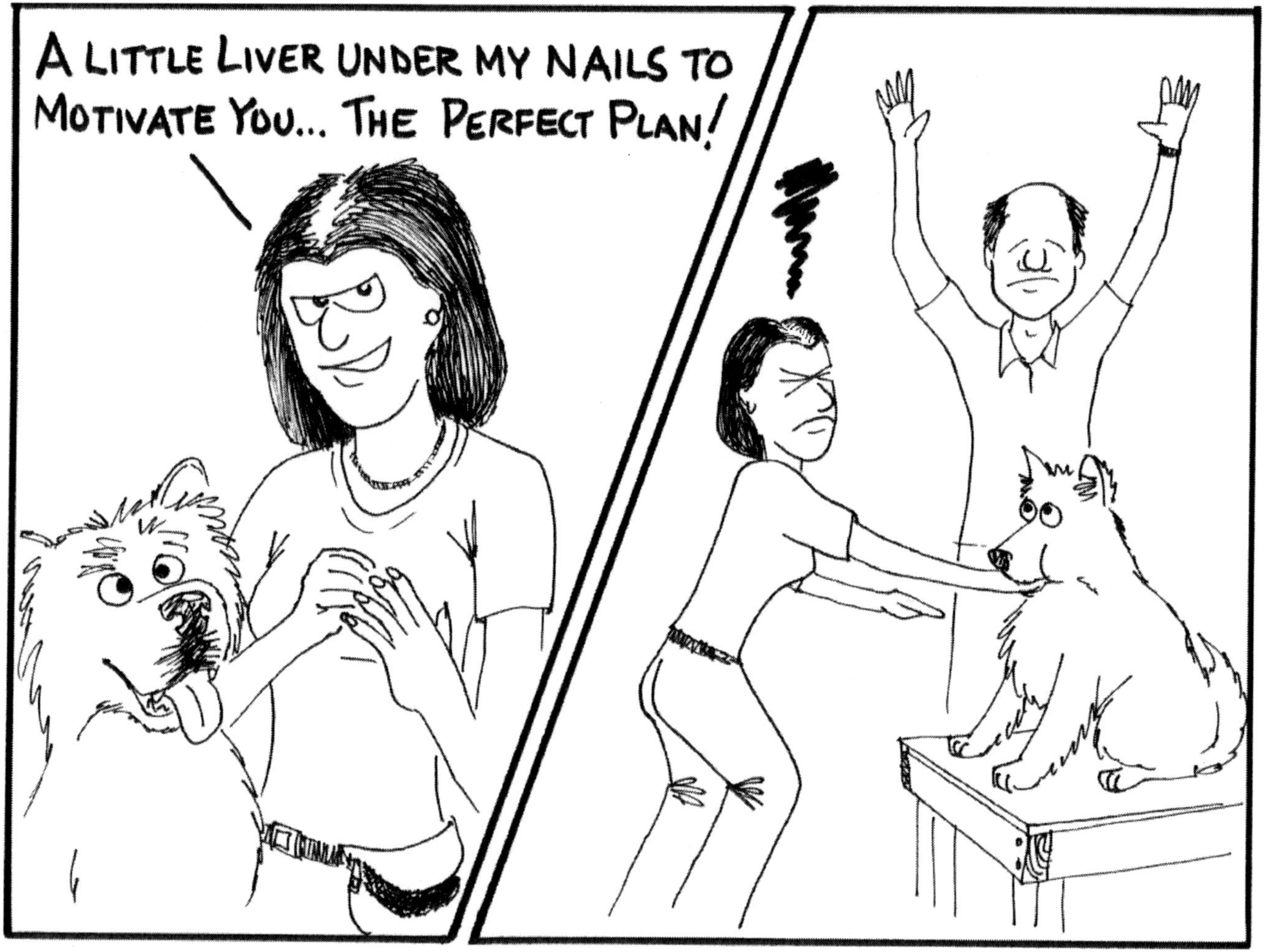
A LITTLE LIVER UNDER MY NAILS TO MOTIVATE YOU... THE PERFECT PLAN!

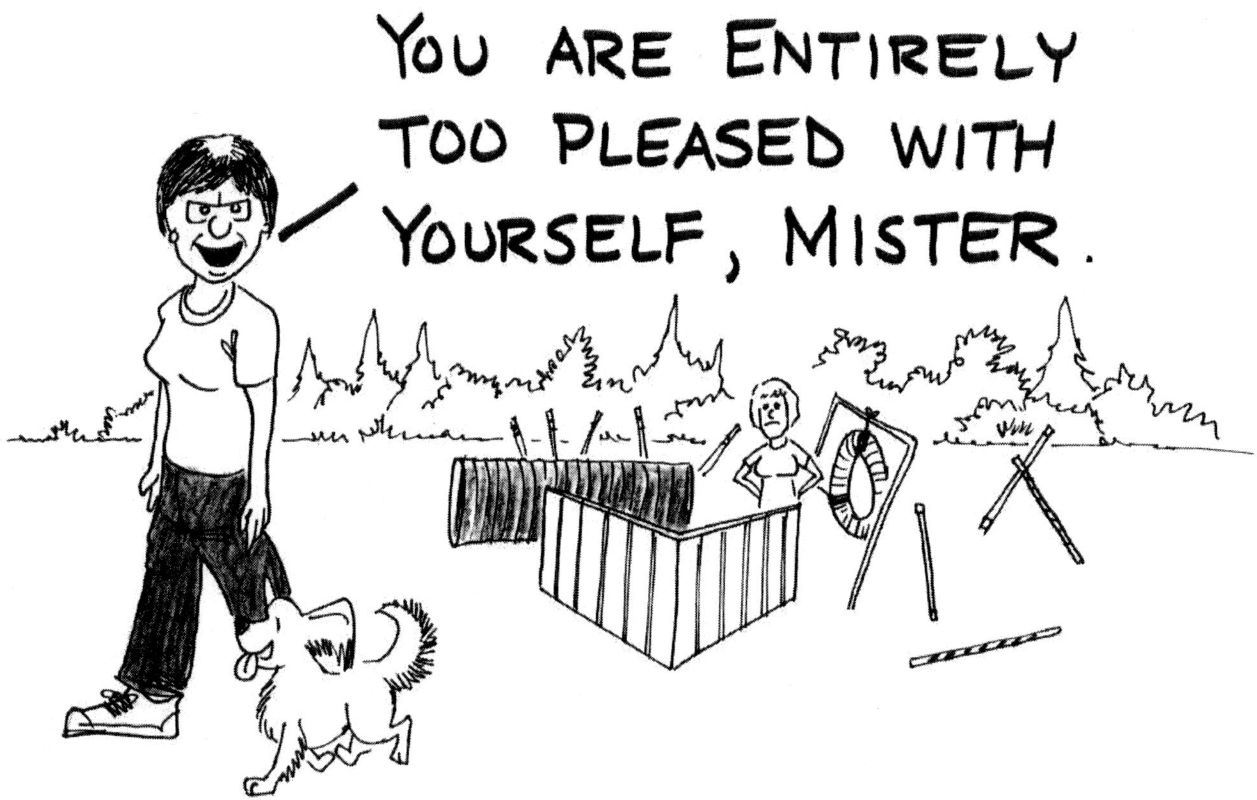
YOU ARE ENTIRELY TOO PLEASED WITH YOURSELF, MISTER.

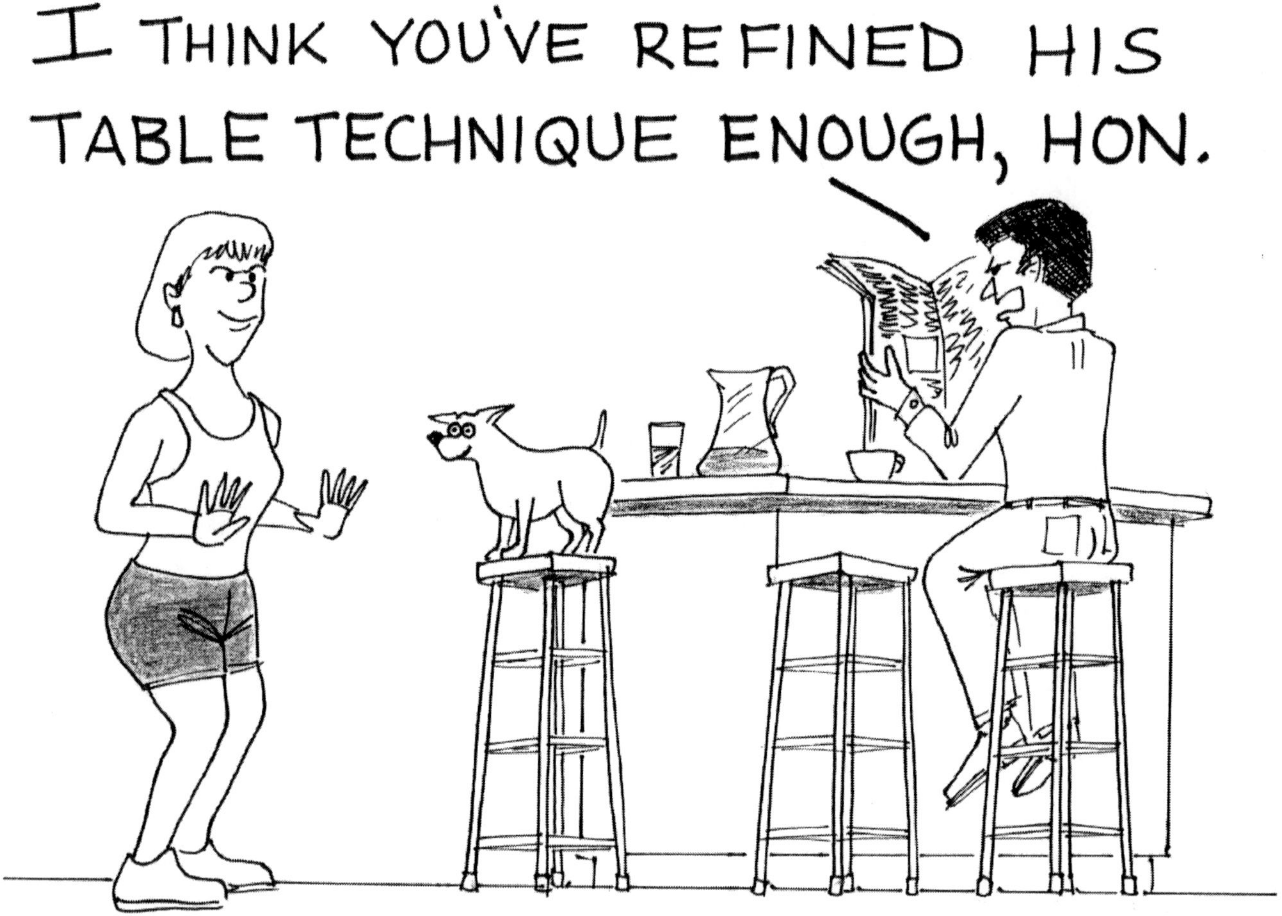
I THINK YOU'VE REFINED HIS TABLE TECHNIQUE ENOUGH, HON.

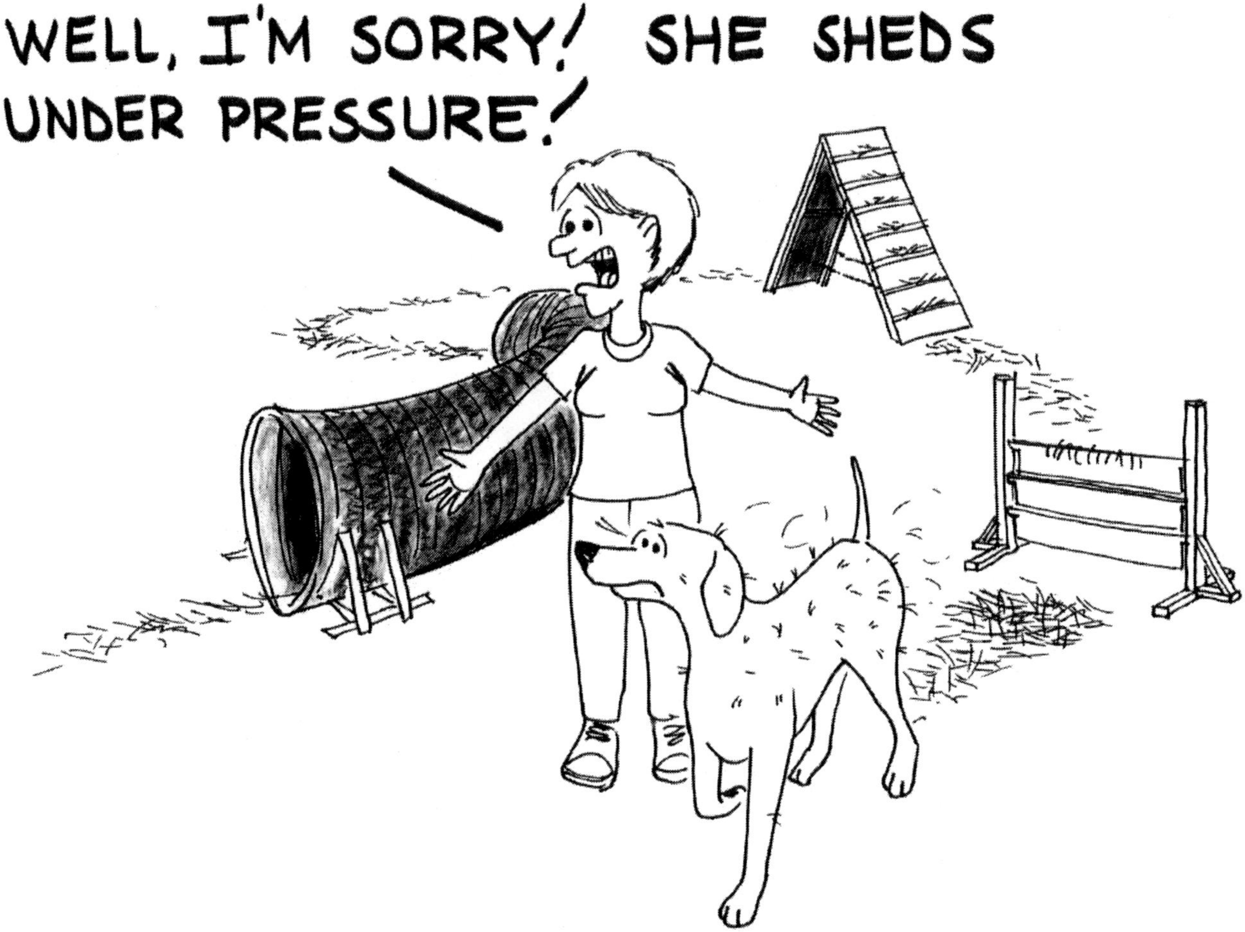
WELL, I'M SORRY! SHE SHEDS UNDER PRESSURE!

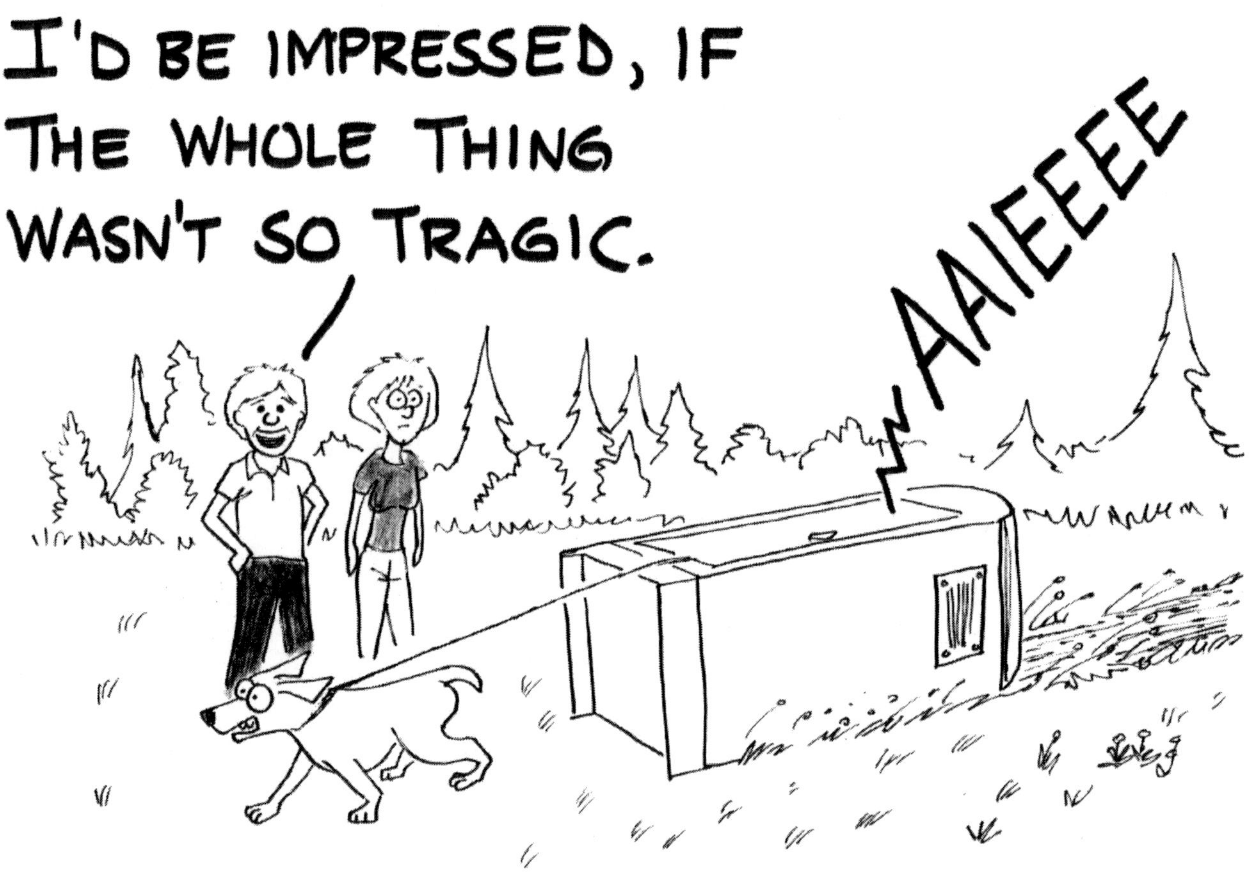
I'D BE IMPRESSED, IF THE WHOLE THING WASN'T SO TRAGIC.
AAIEEEE

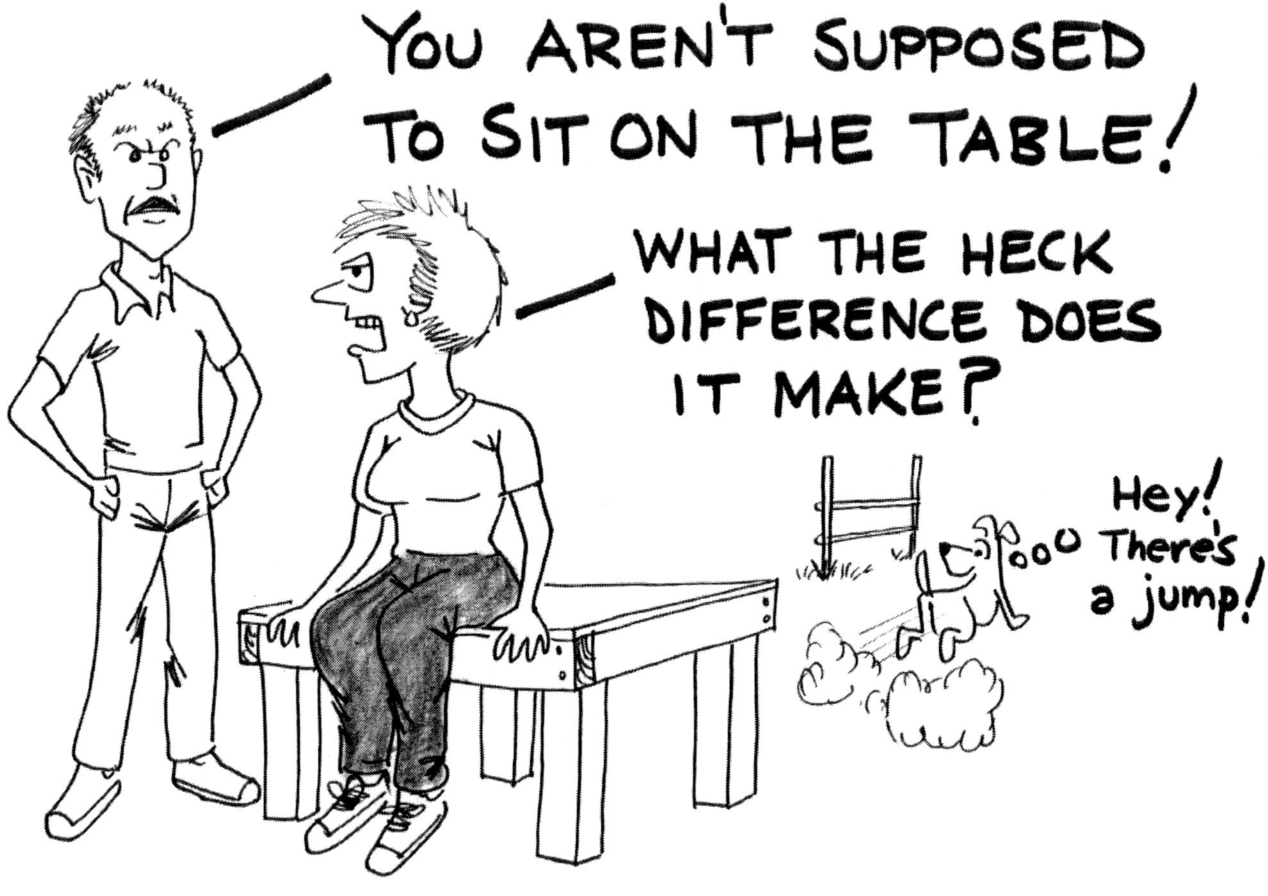
YOU AREN'T SUPPOSED TO SIT ON THE TABLE!
WHAT THE HECK DIFFERENCE DOES IT MAKE?
Hey! There's a jump!

OOOPS.

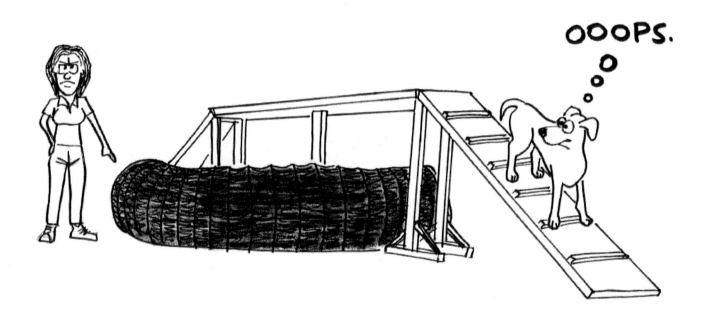

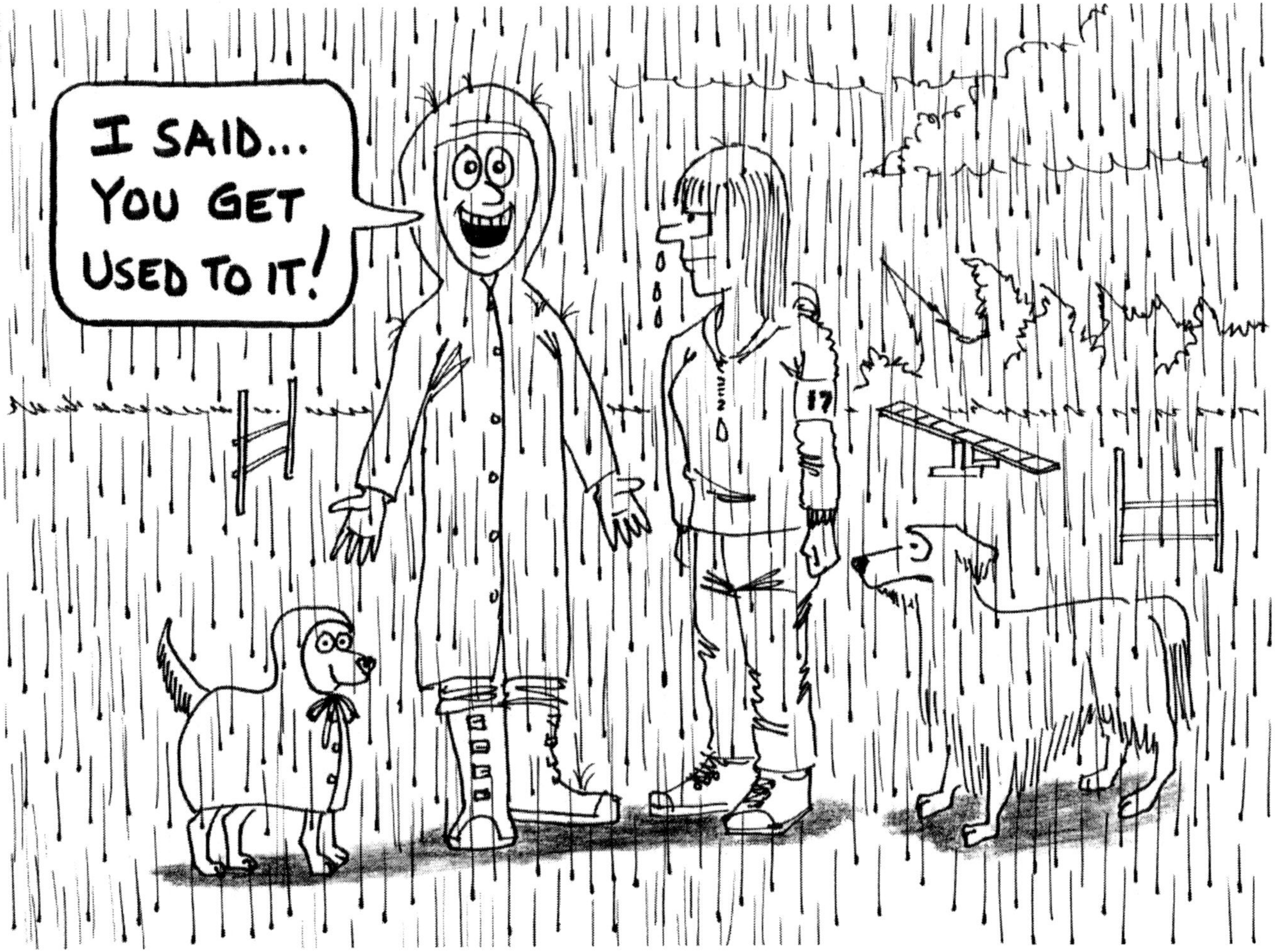
I SAID...
YOU GET
USED TO IT!
17

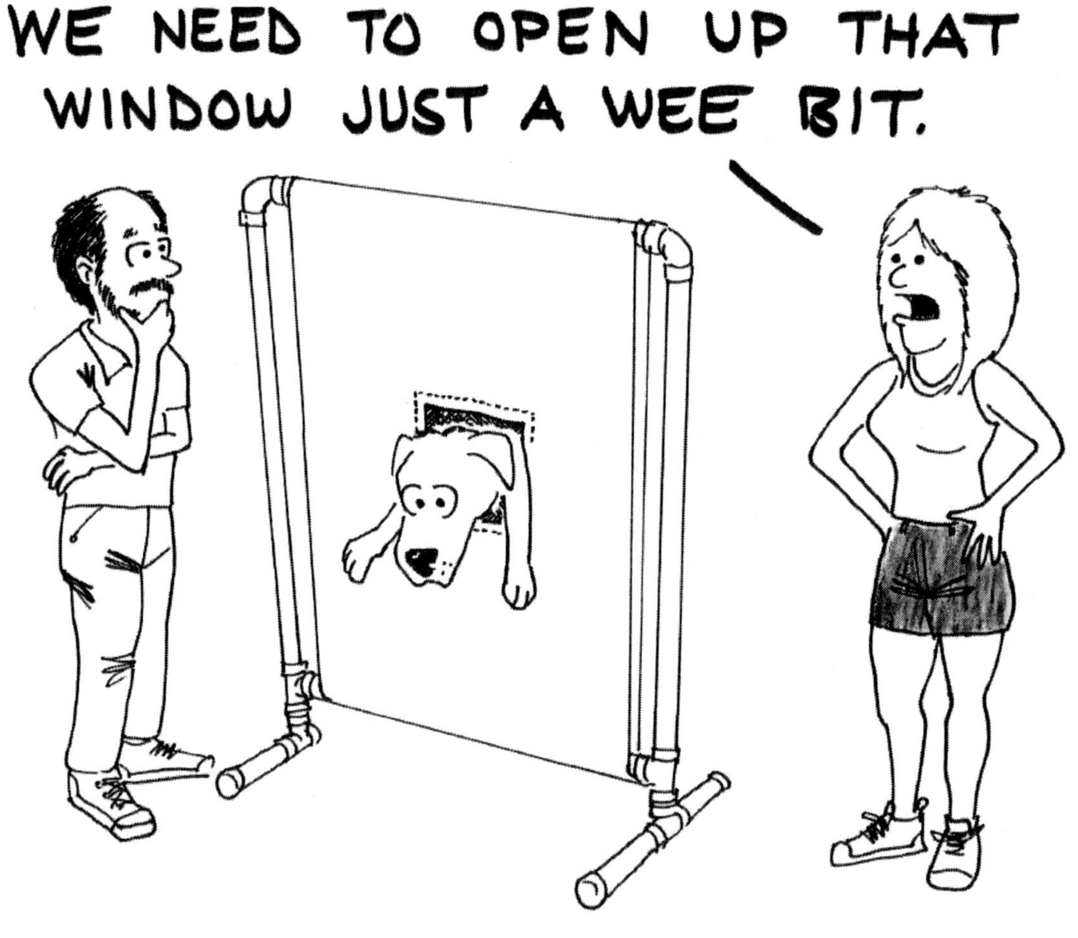
WE NEED TO OPEN UP THAT WINDOW JUST A WEE BIT.

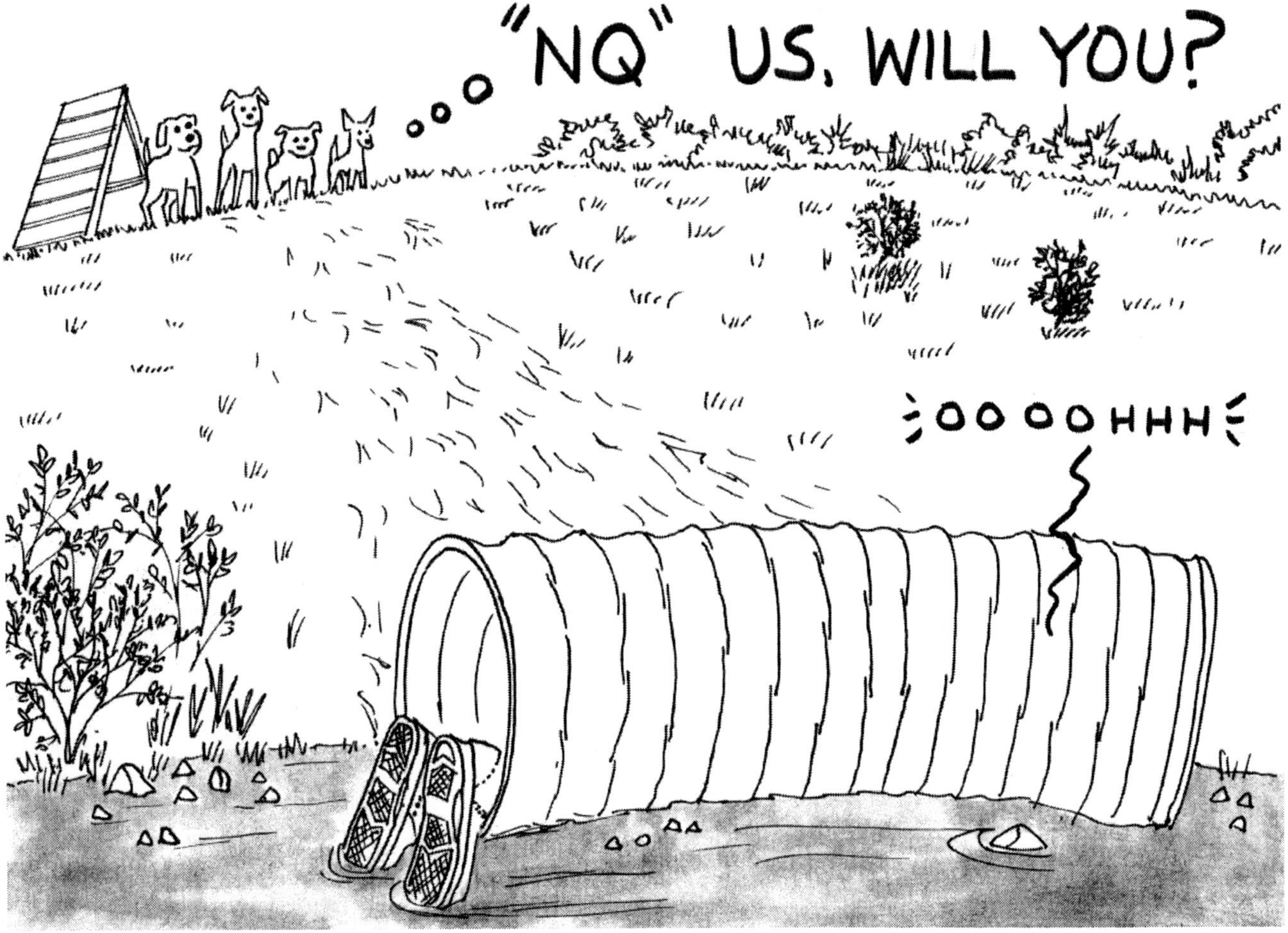
"NQ" US, WILL YOU?
OOOOHHH

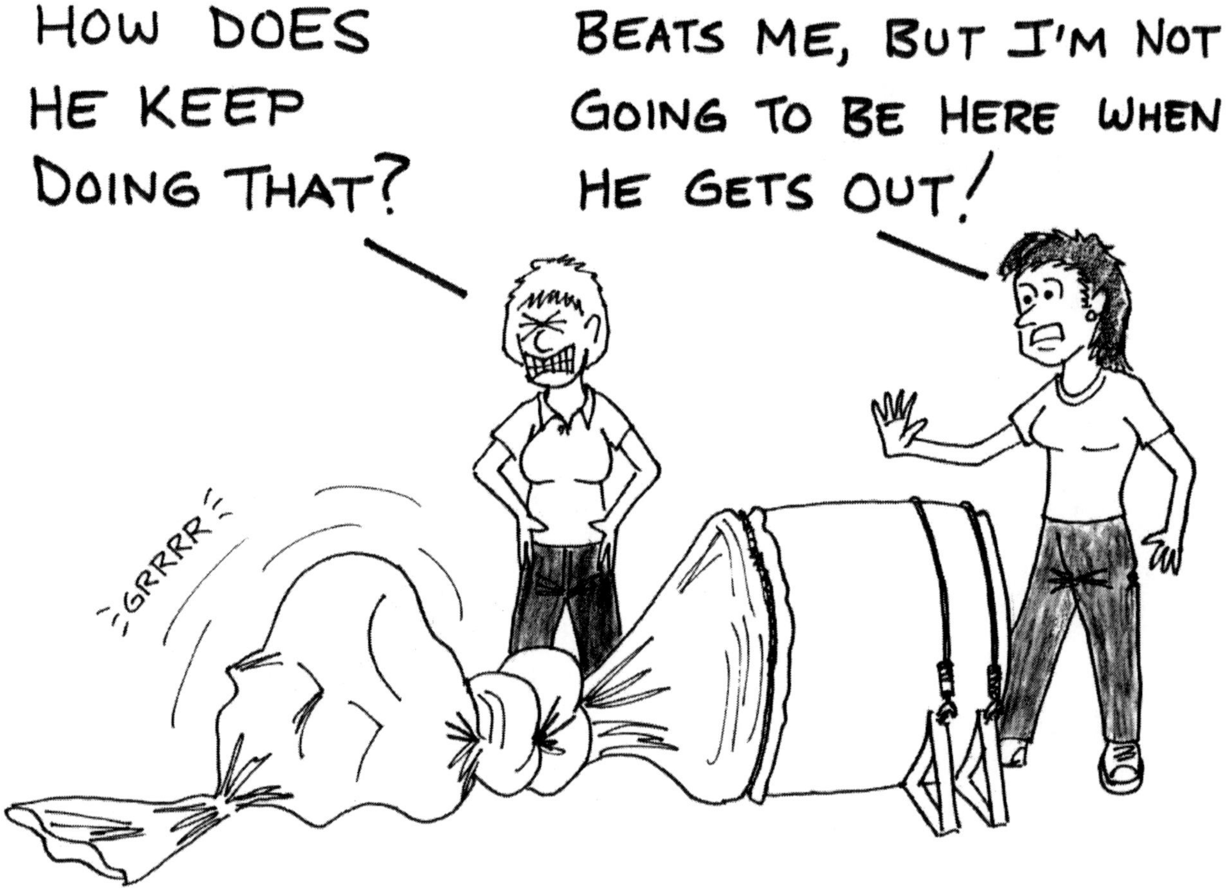

HOW DOES HE KEEP DOING THAT?
BEATS ME, BUT I'M NOT GOING TO BE HERE WHEN HE GETS OUT!
GRRRR

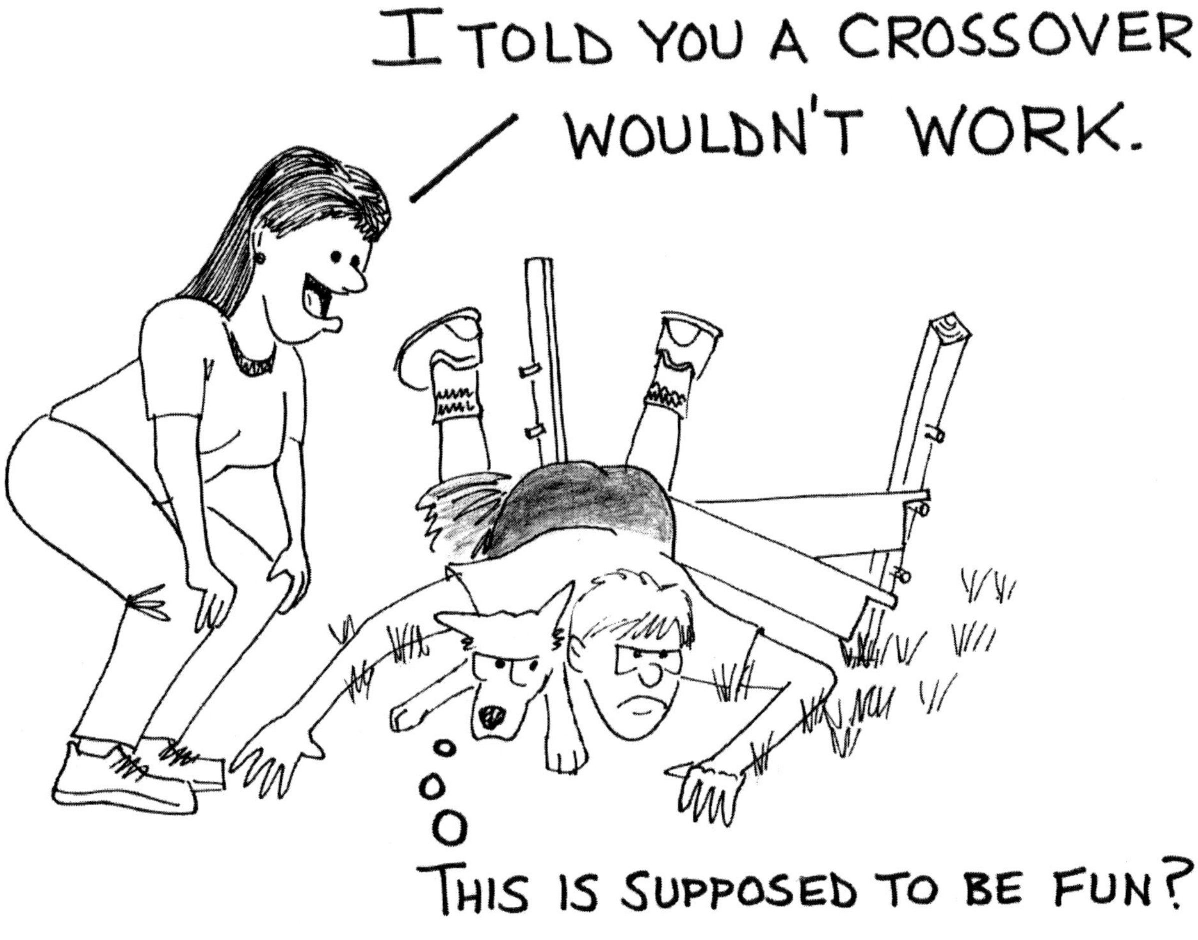
I TOLD YOU A CROSSOVER WOULDN'T WORK.
THIS IS SUPPOSED TO BE FUN?

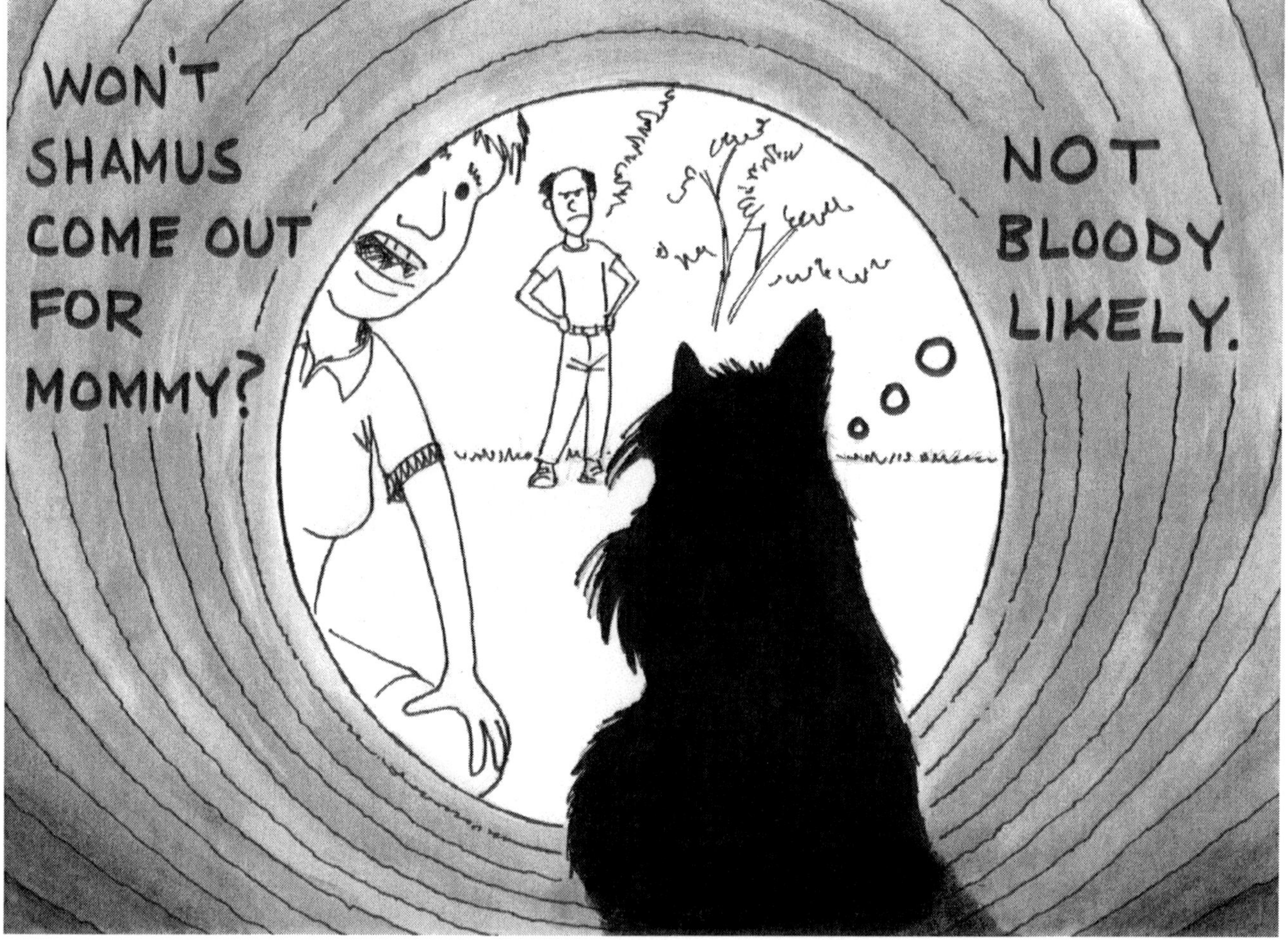
WON'T SHAMUS COME OUT FOR MOMMY?
NOT BLOODY LIKELY.

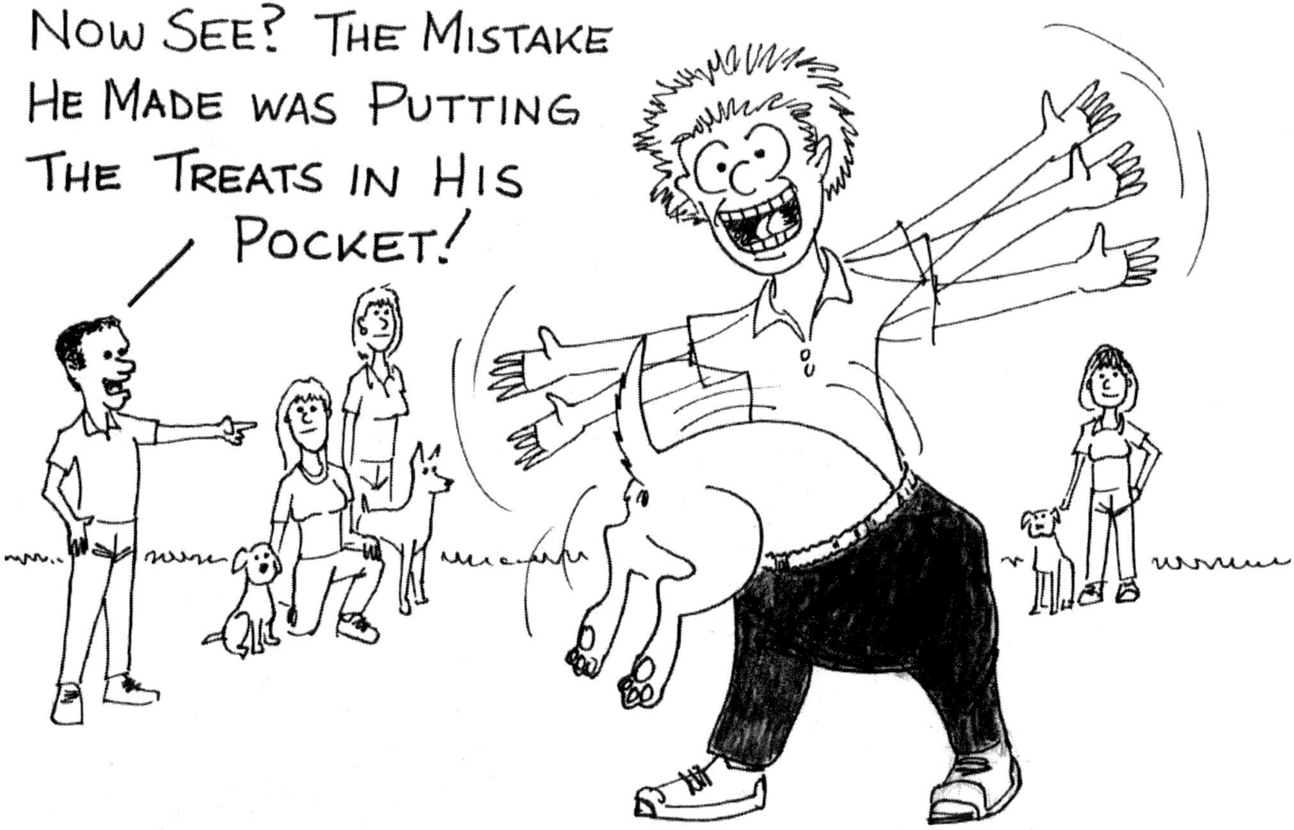
NOW SEE? THE MISTAKE HE MADE WAS PUTTING THE TREATS IN HIS POCKET!

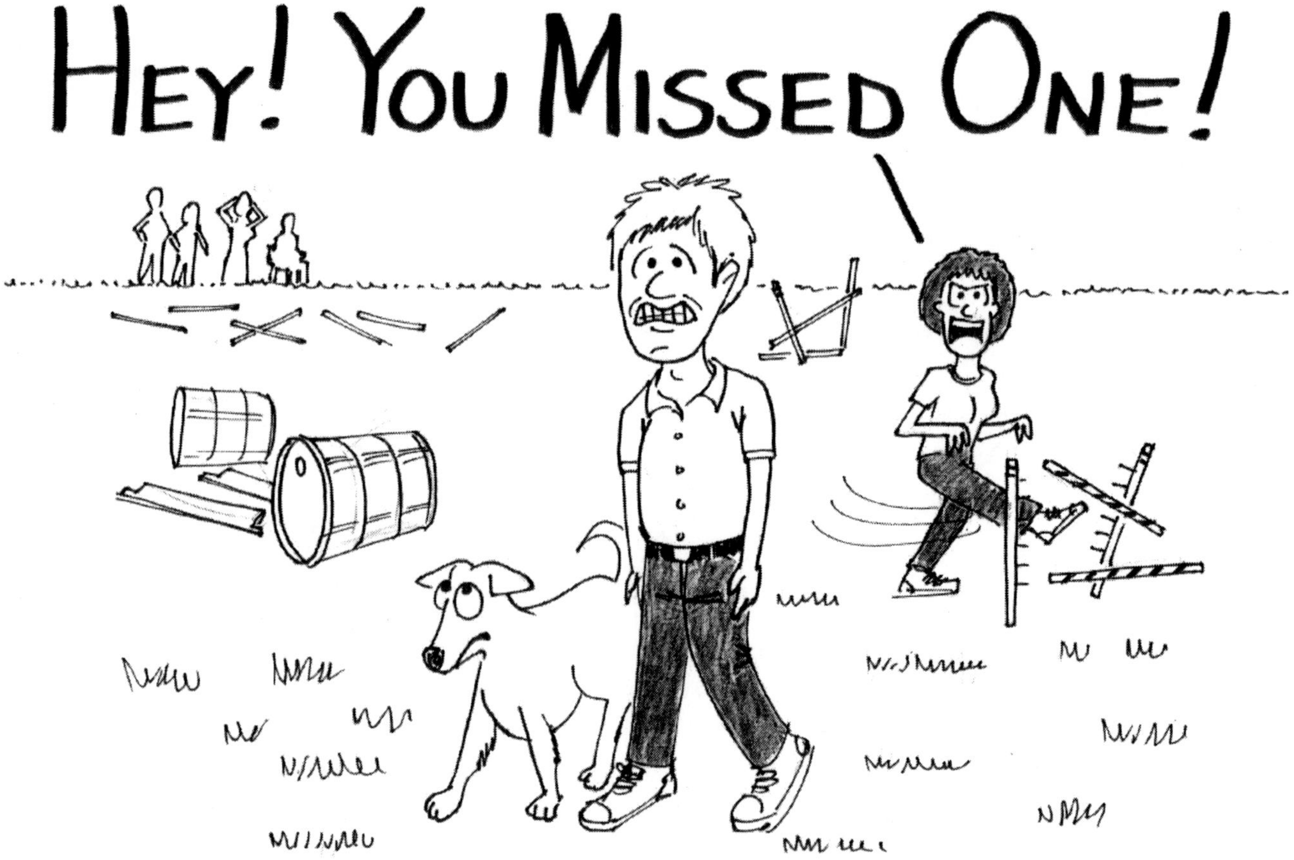
HEY! YOU MISSED ONE!

≥AHEM≤
YOU WERE
SAYING
SOMETHING
ABOUT
A "TREAT"?

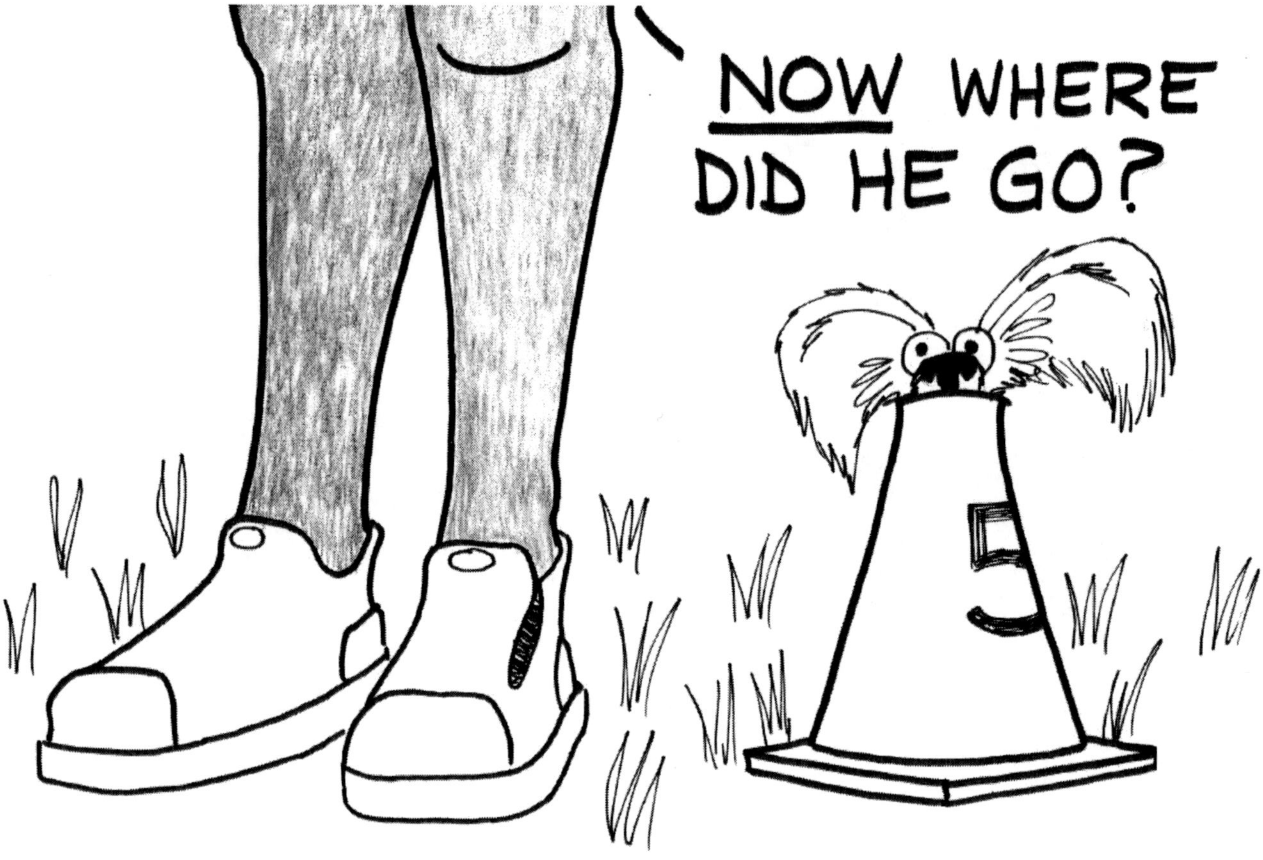
NOW WHERE DID HE GO?
5

YOU KNOW, AGILITY AND OBEDIENCE ARE **NOT** MUTUALLY EXCLUSIVE ACTIVITIES.

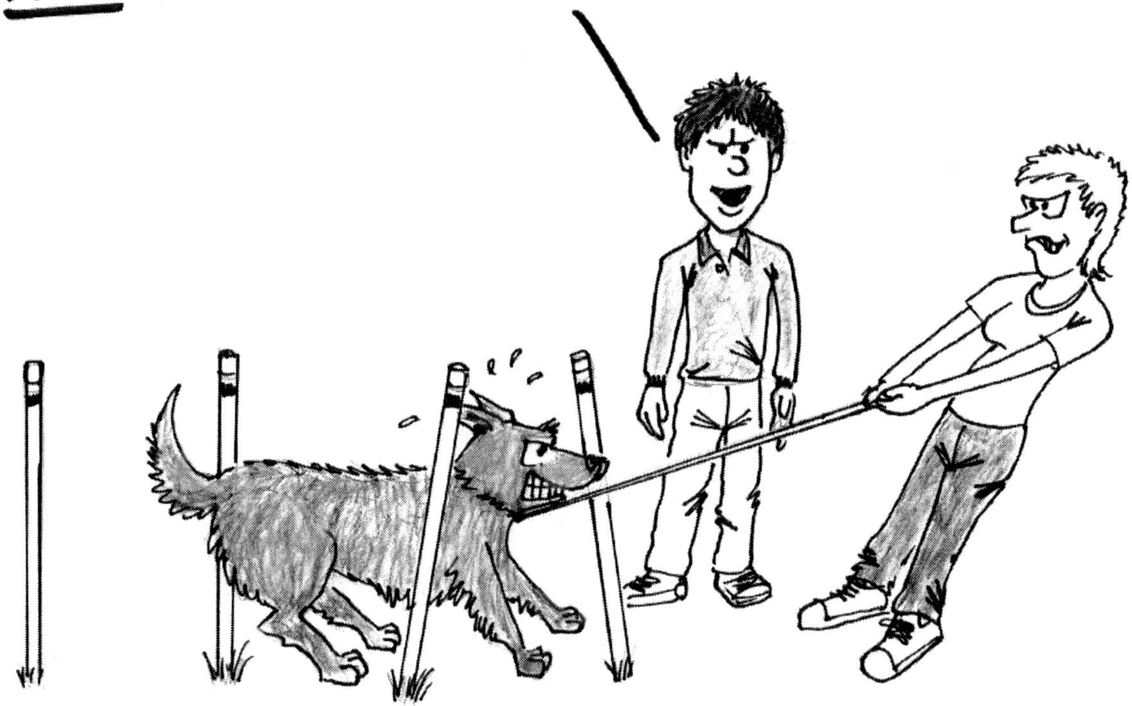

YOU'RE GONNA NEED TO START GETTING THOSE COMMANDS OUT SOONER.
7

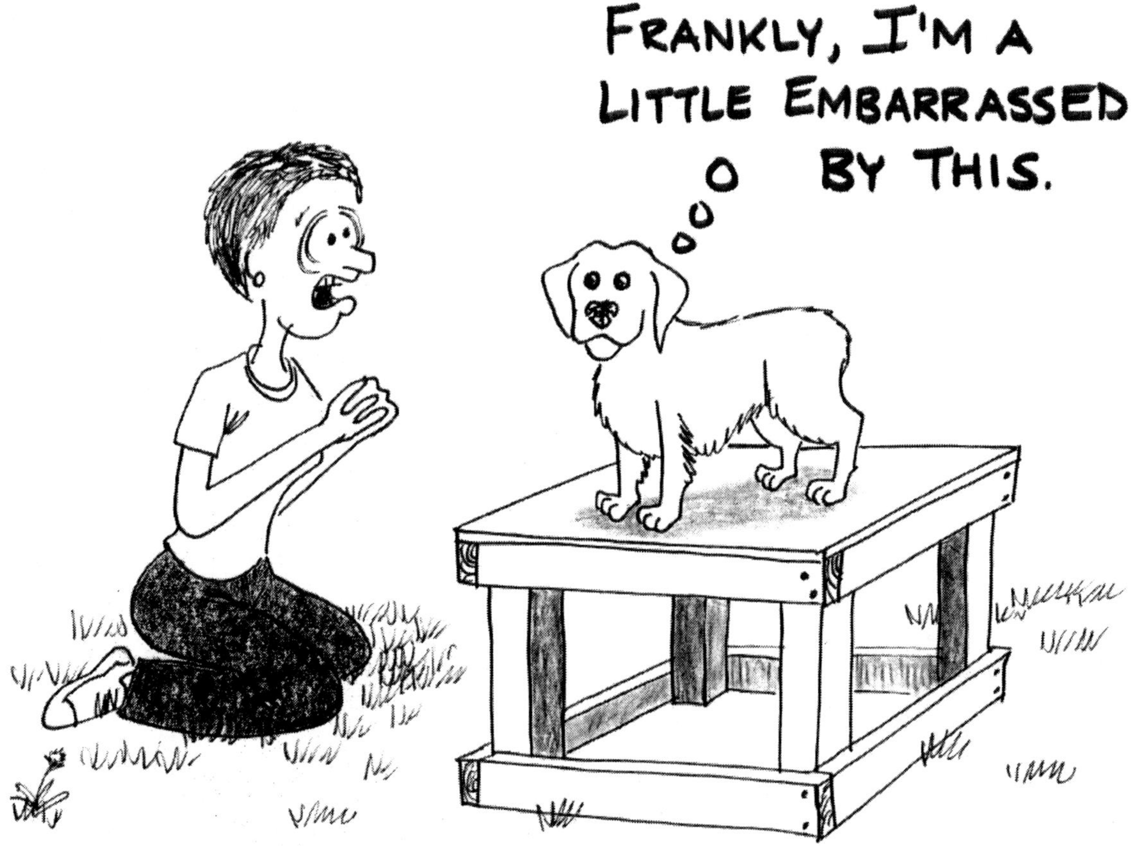
FRANKLY, I'M A LITTLE EMBARRASSED BY THIS.

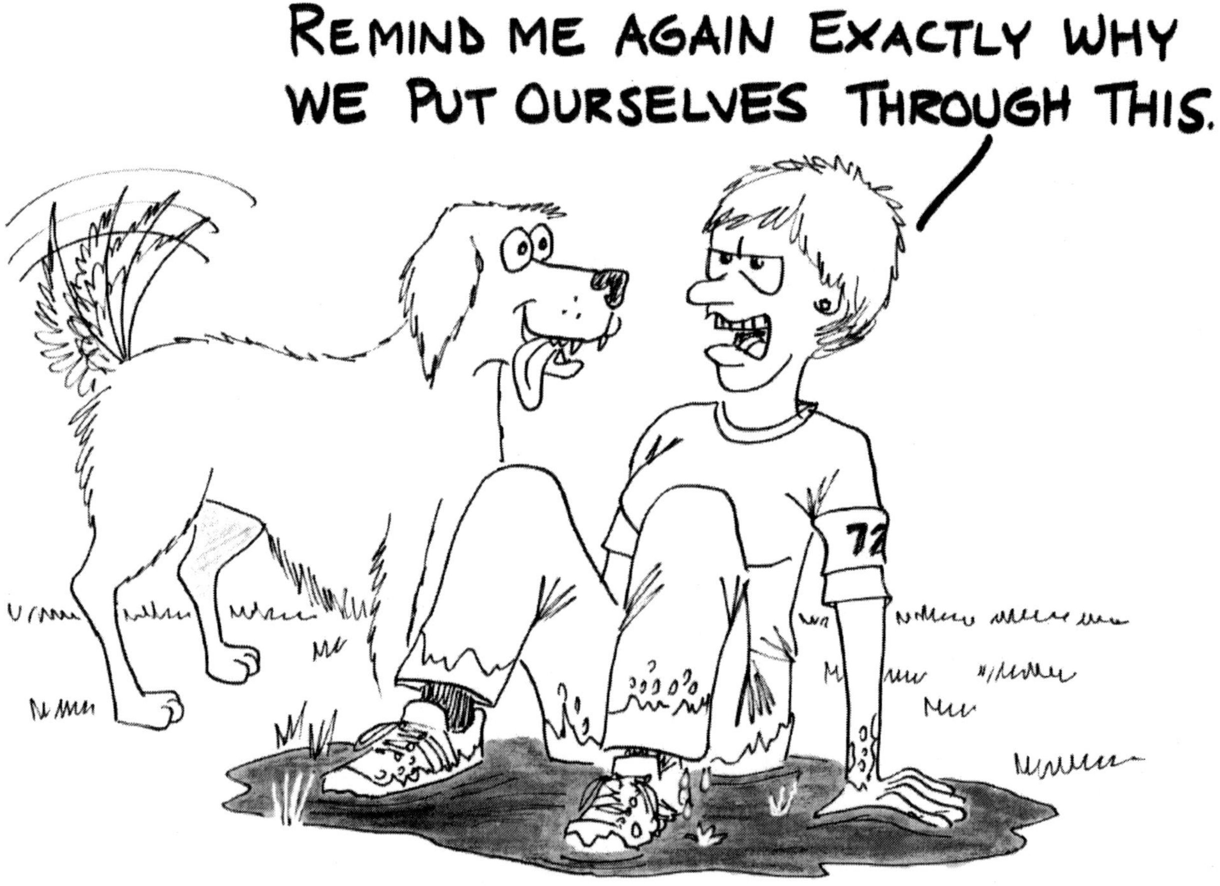
REMIND ME AGAIN EXACTLY WHY WE PUT OURSELVES THROUGH THIS.
72

OH, SWELL...HORIZONTAL WEAVE POLES.

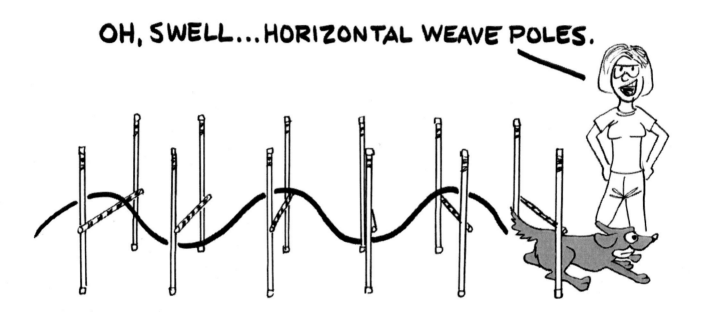

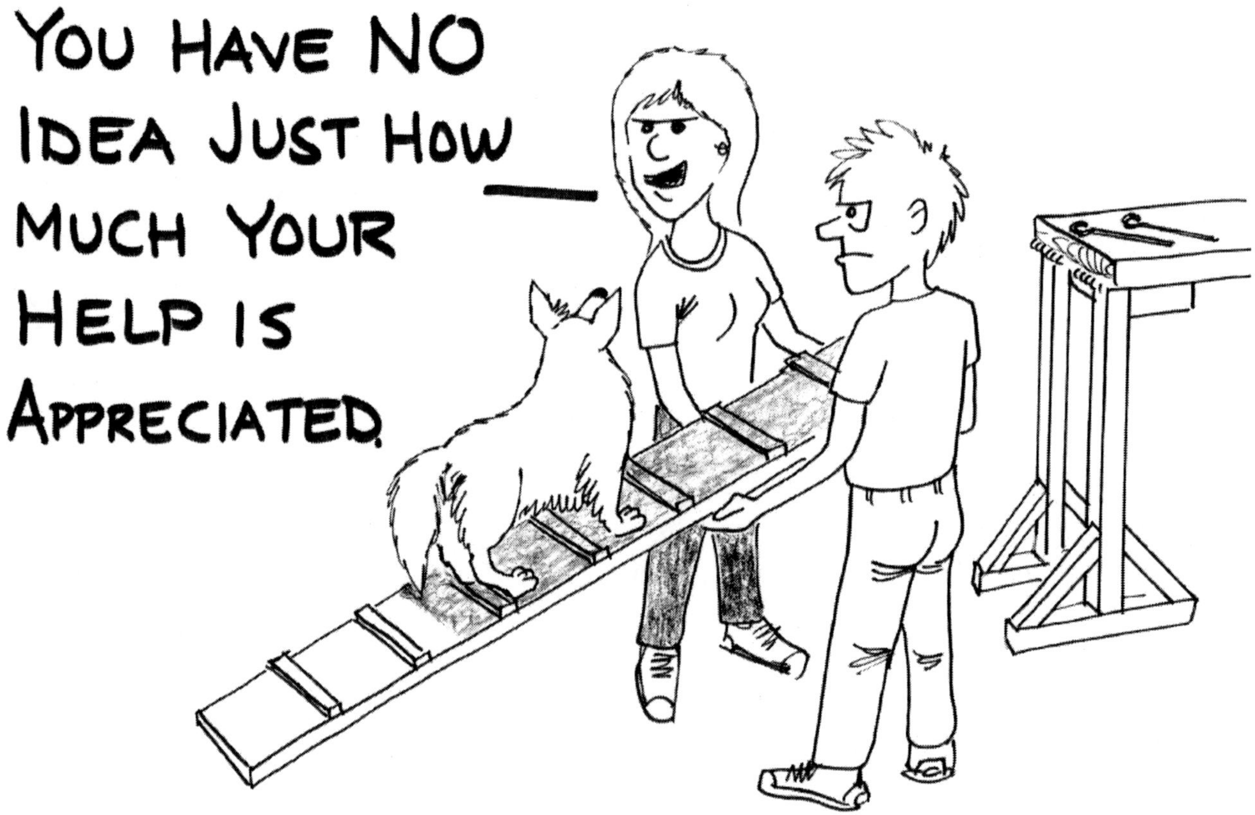
YOU HAVE NO IDEA JUST HOW MUCH YOUR HELP IS APPRECIATED.

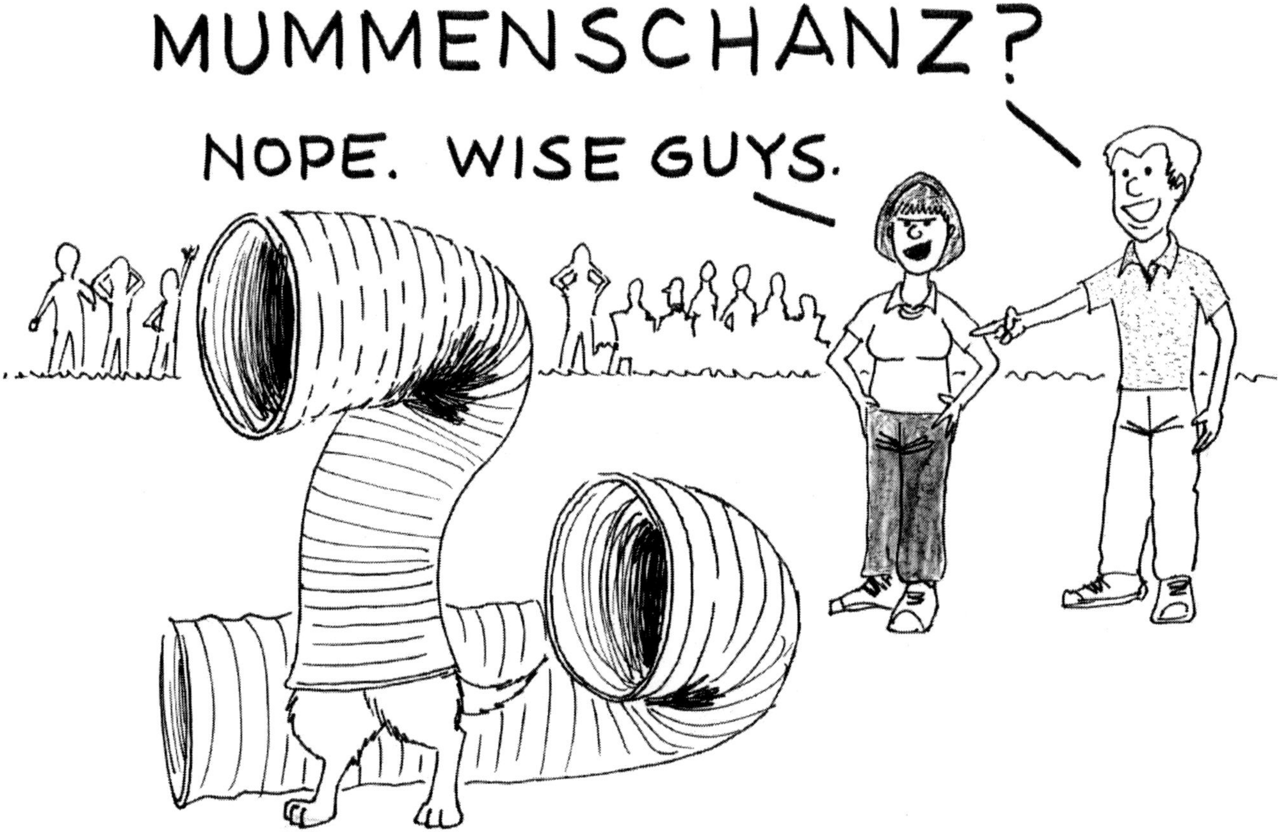
MUMMENSCHANZ?
NOPE. WISE GUYS.

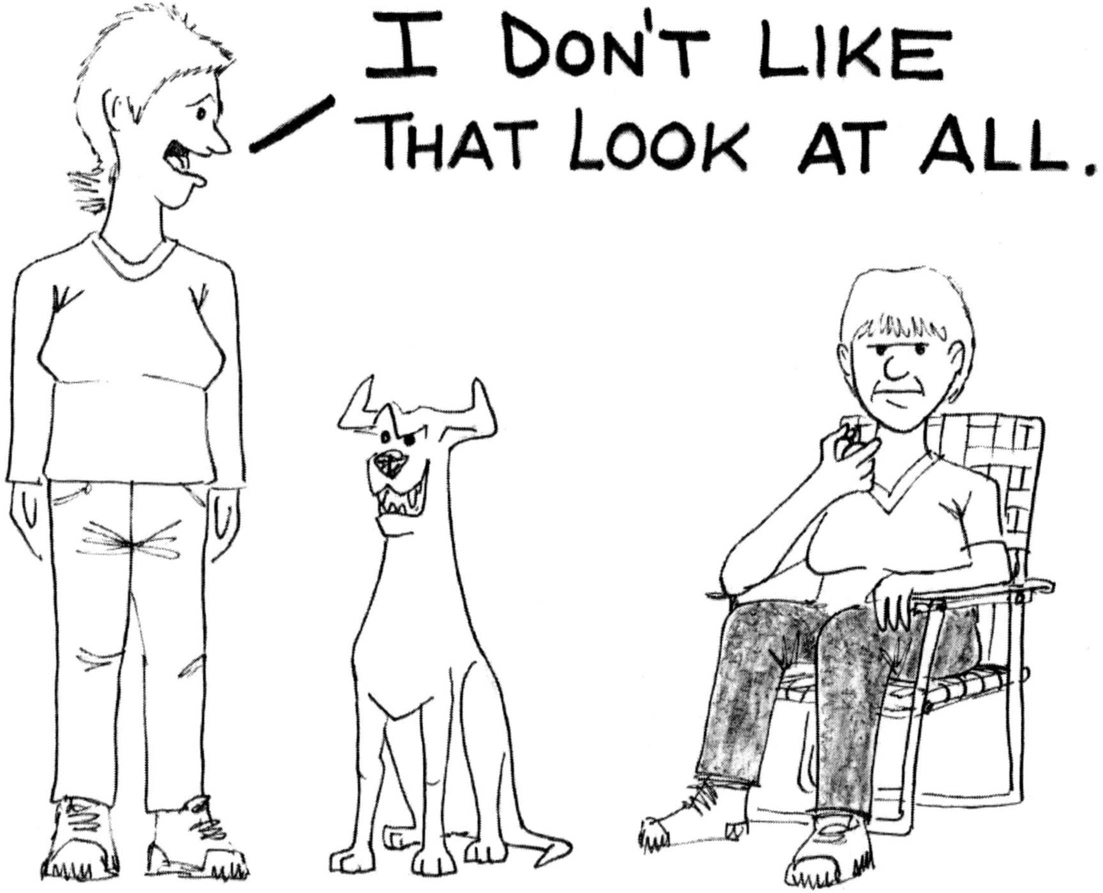
I DON'T LIKE THAT LOOK AT ALL.

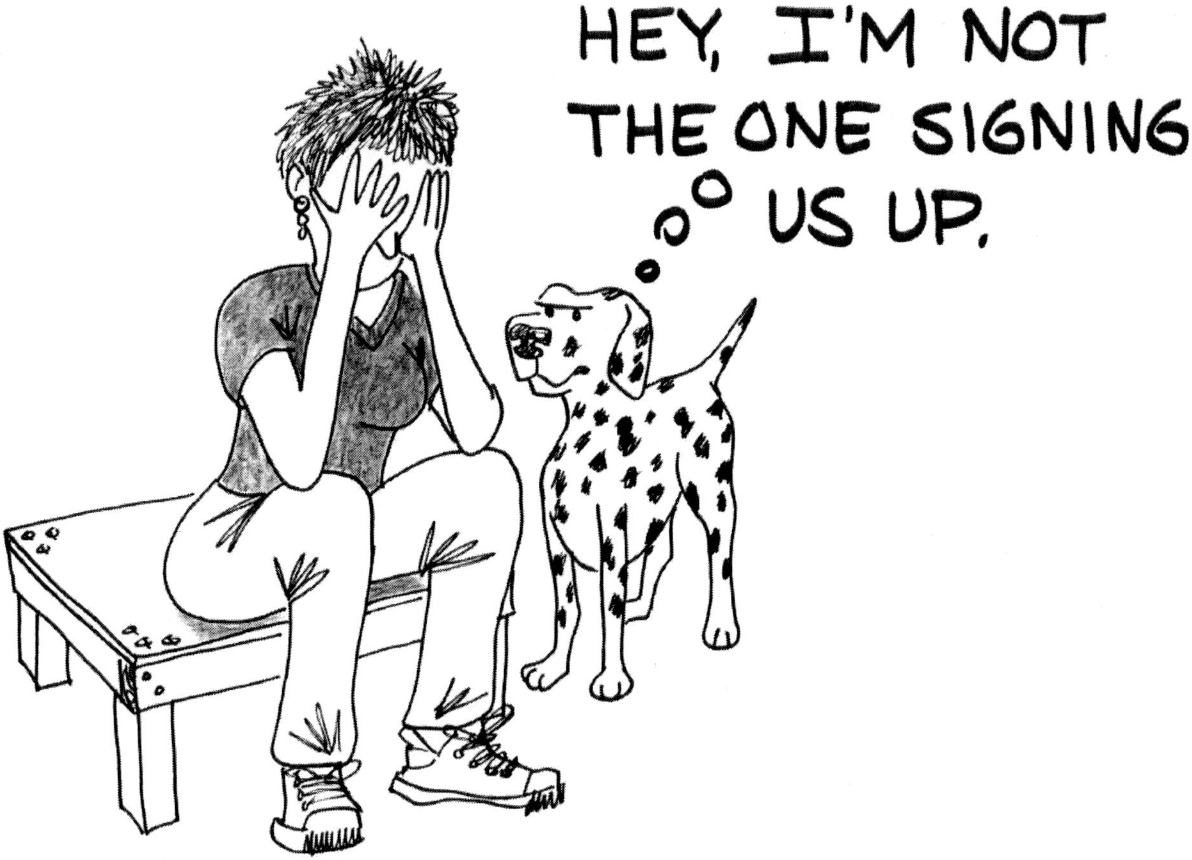
HEY, I'M NOT THE ONE SIGNING US UP.

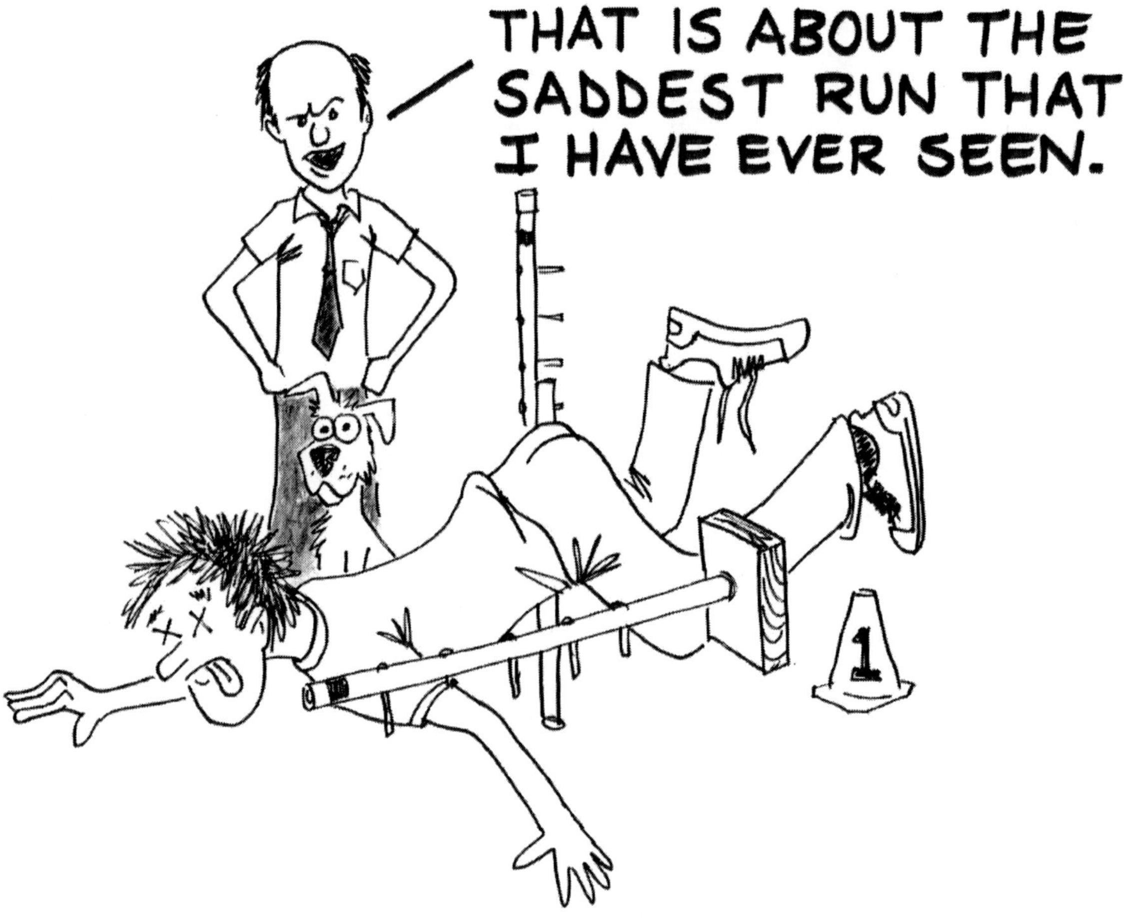
THAT IS ABOUT THE SADDEST RUN THAT I HAVE EVER SEEN.
1

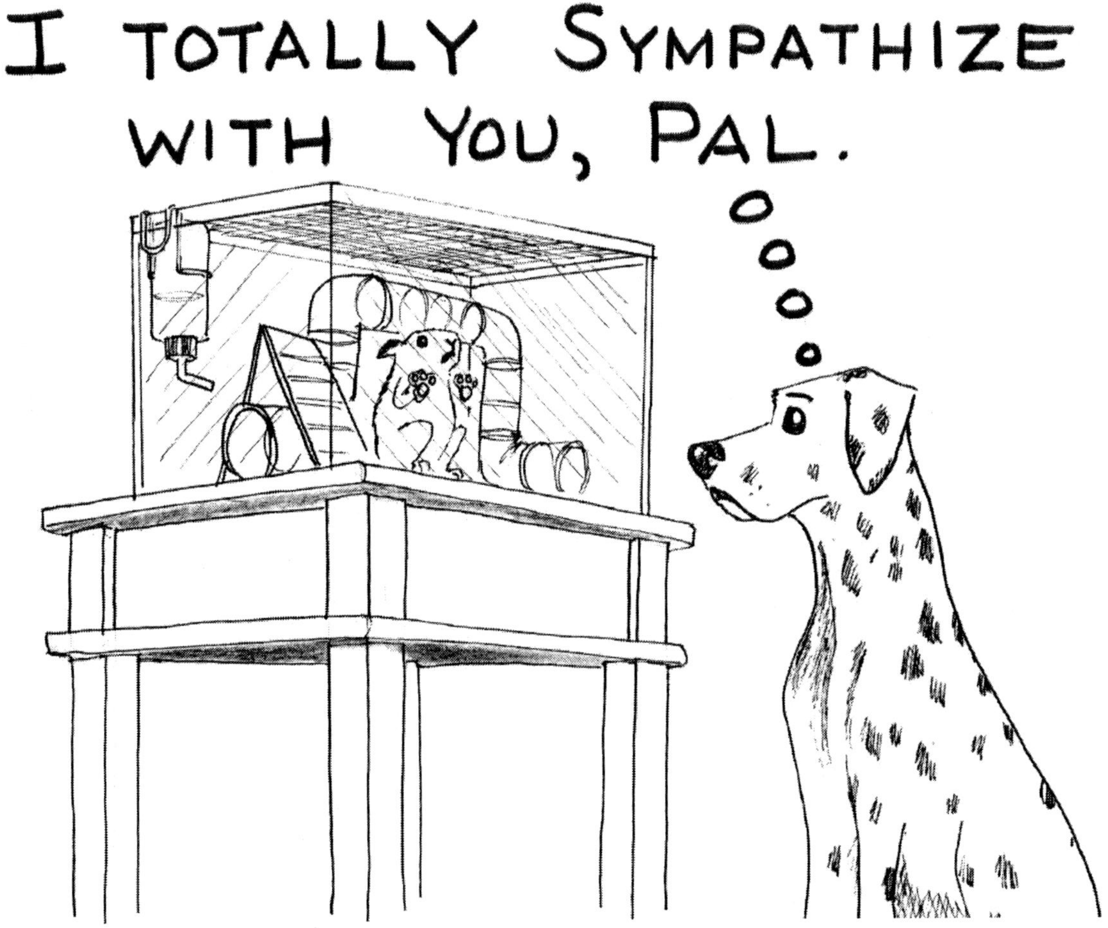
I TOTALLY SYMPATHIZE WITH YOU, PAL.

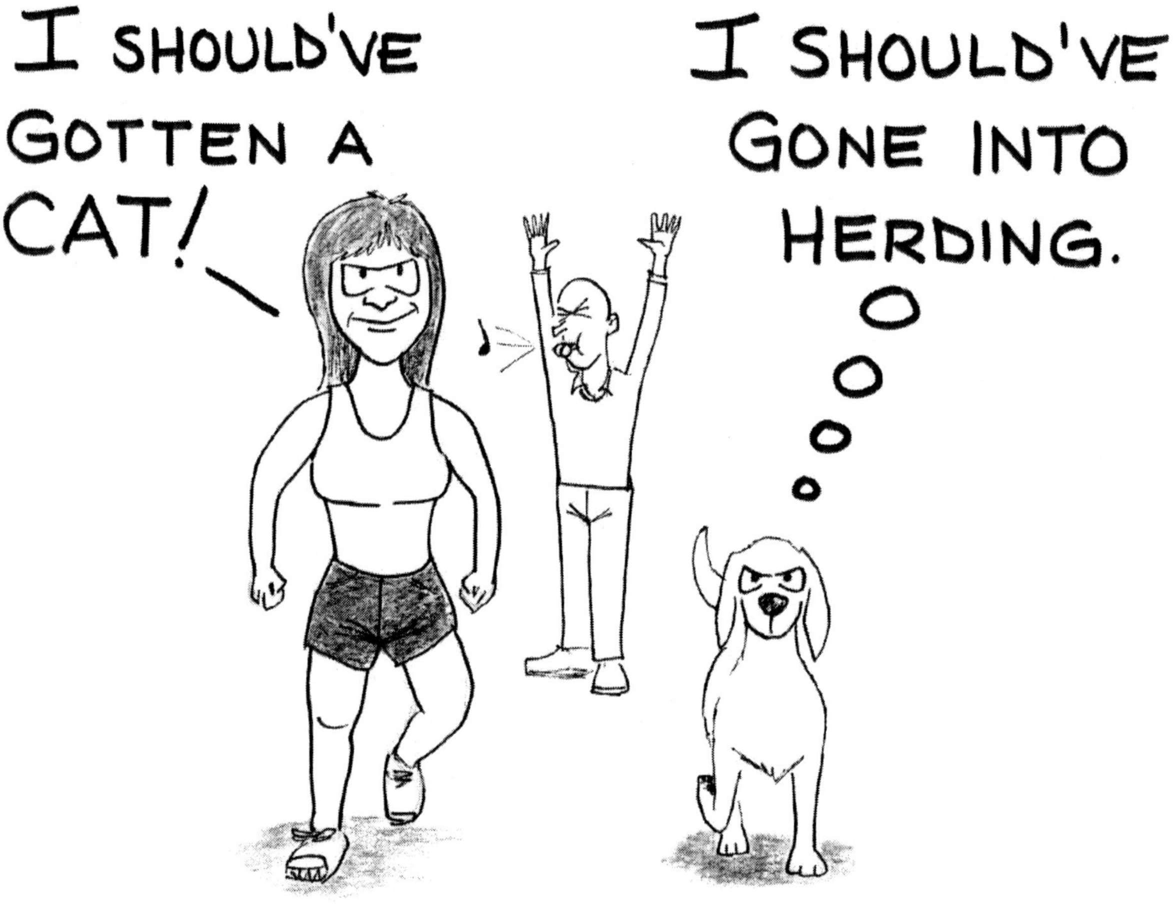
I SHOULD'VE GOTTEN A CAT!
I SHOULD'VE GONE INTO HERDING.

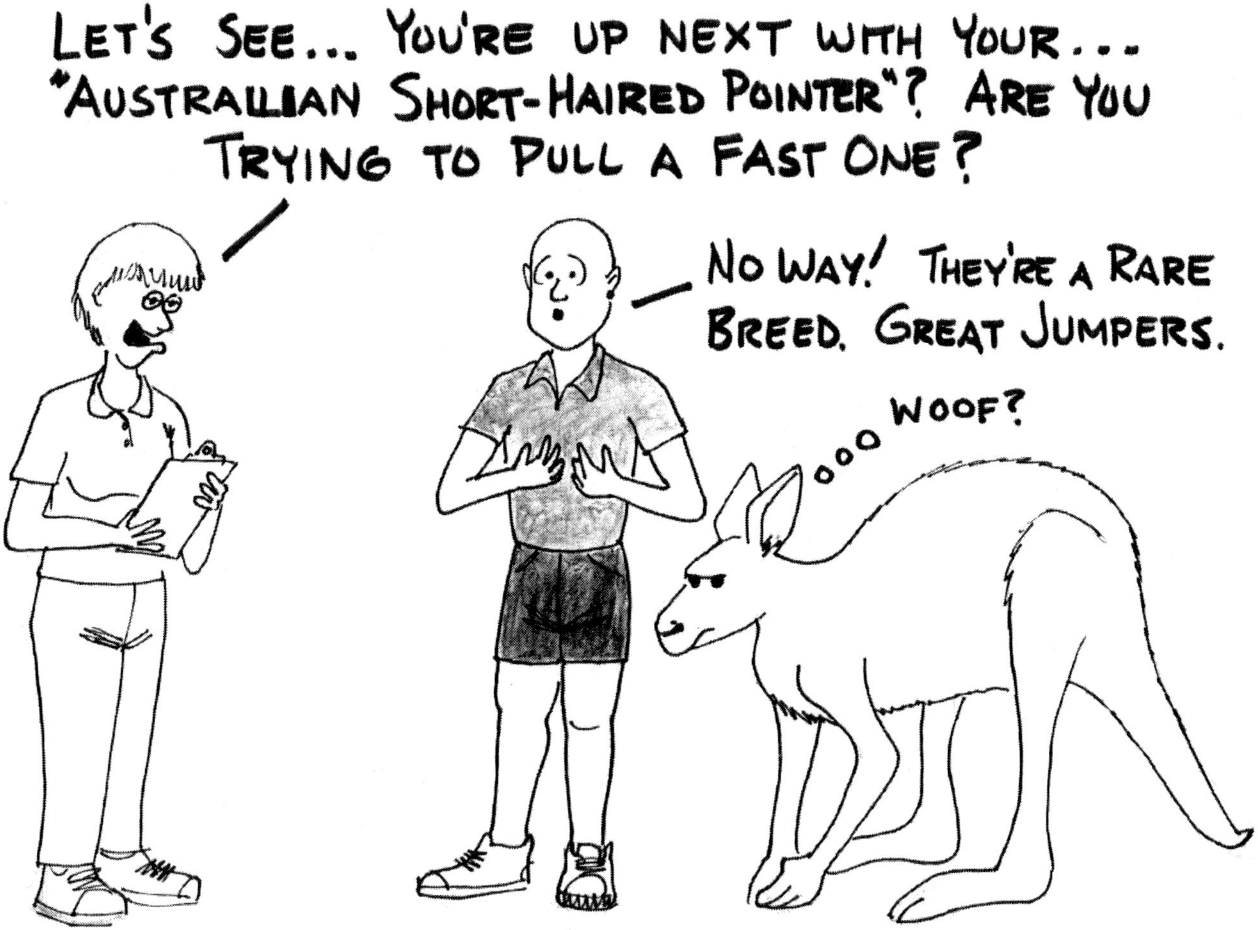
LET'S SEE... YOU'RE UP NEXT WITH YOUR... "AUSTRALLIAN SHORT-HAIRED POINTER"? ARE YOU TRYING TO PULL A FAST ONE?
NO WAY! THEY'RE A RARE BREED. GREAT JUMPERS.
WOOF?

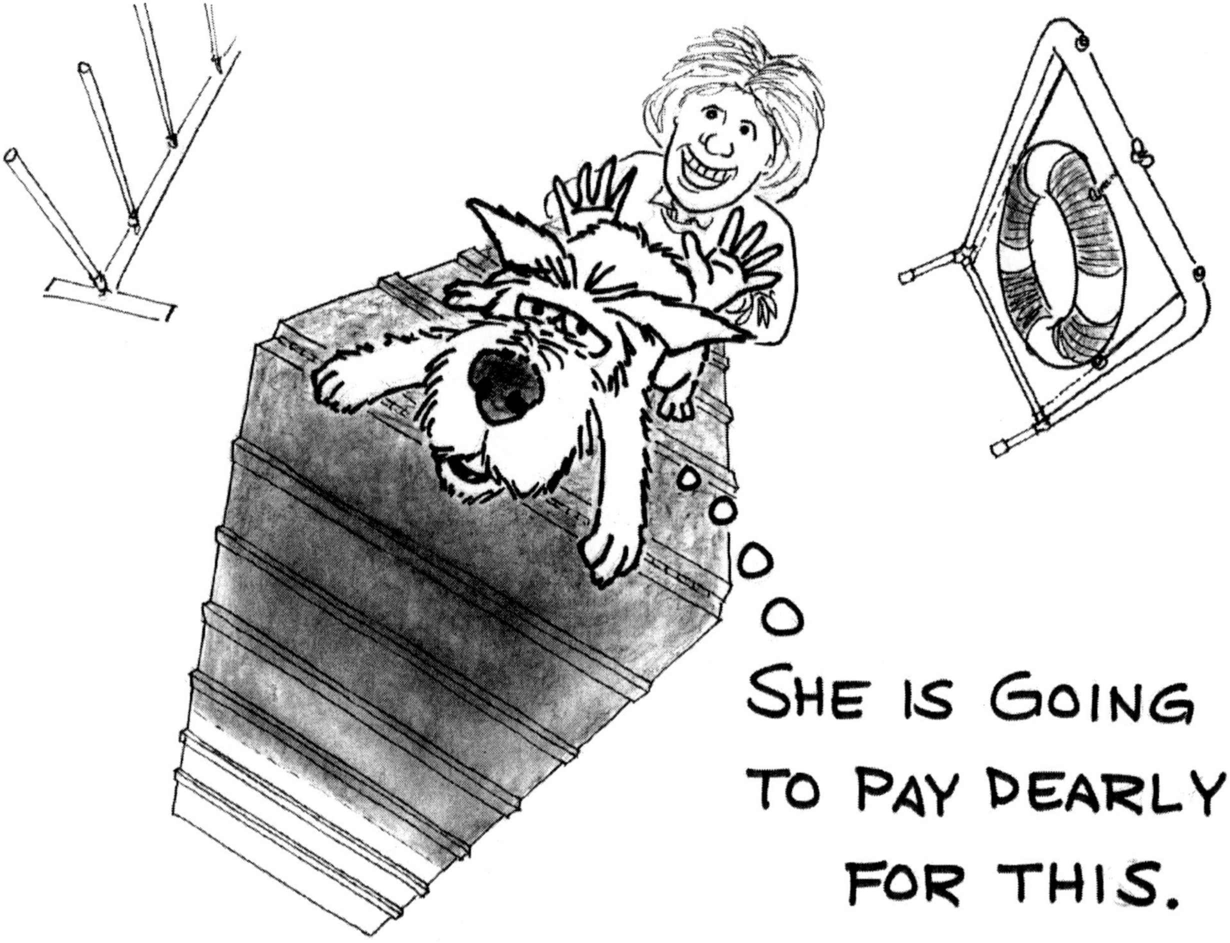
SHE IS GOING
TO PAY DEARLY
FOR THIS.

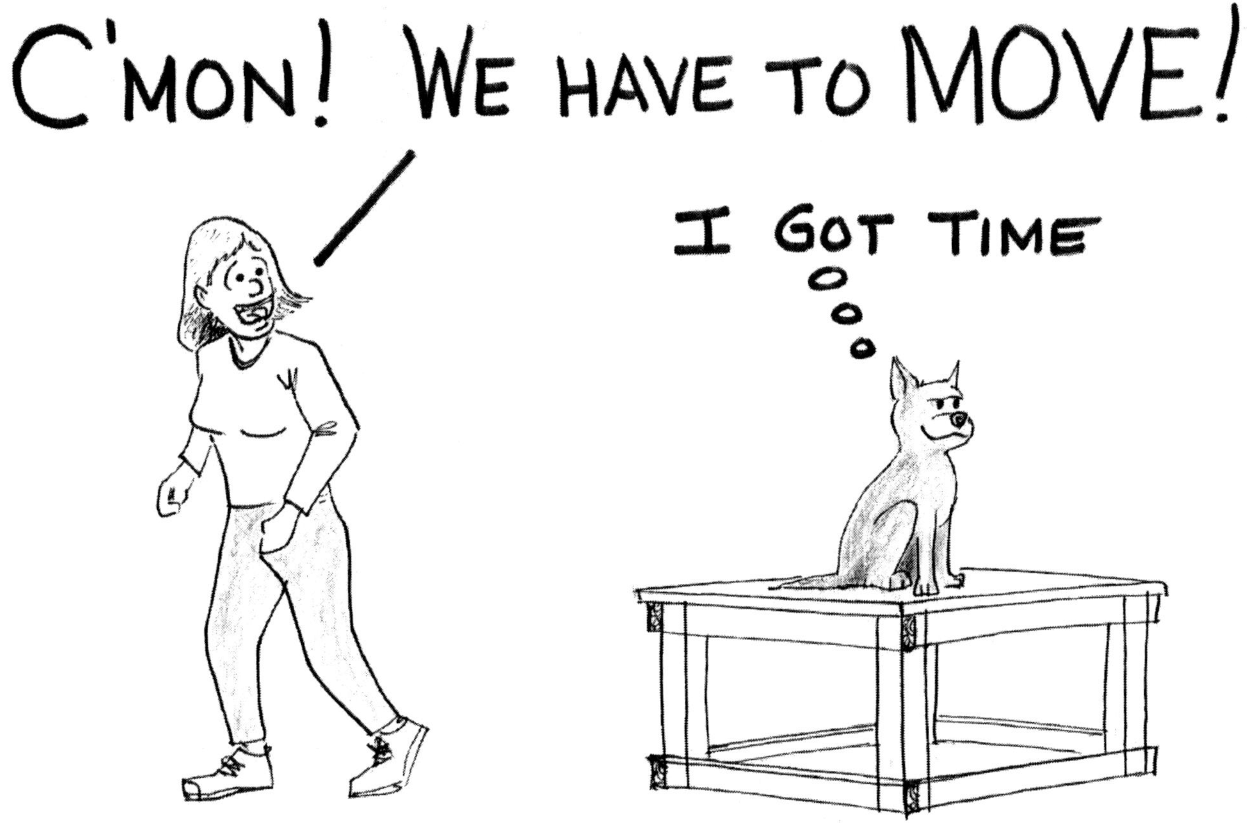
C'MON! WE HAVE TO MOVE!
I GOT TIME

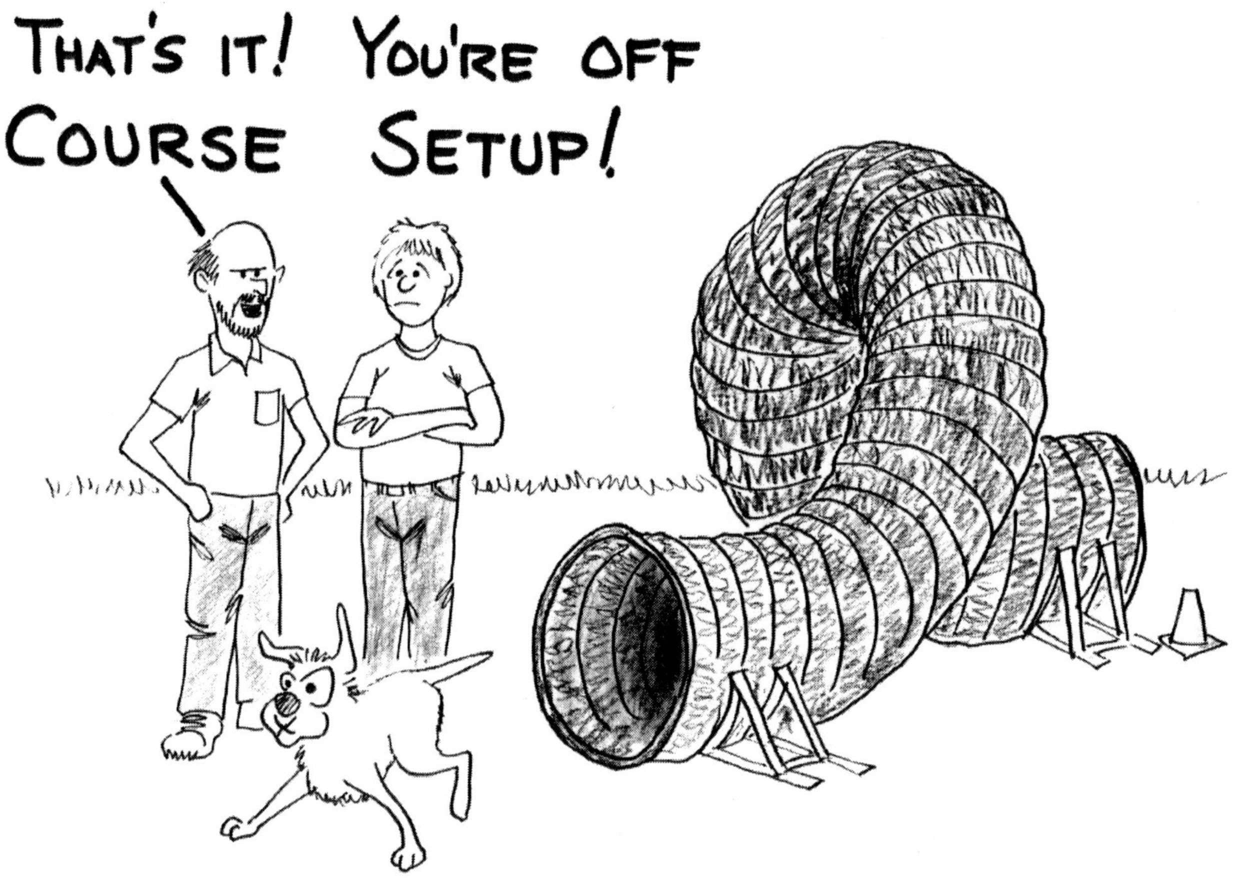
THAT'S IT! YOU'RE OFF COURSE SETUP!

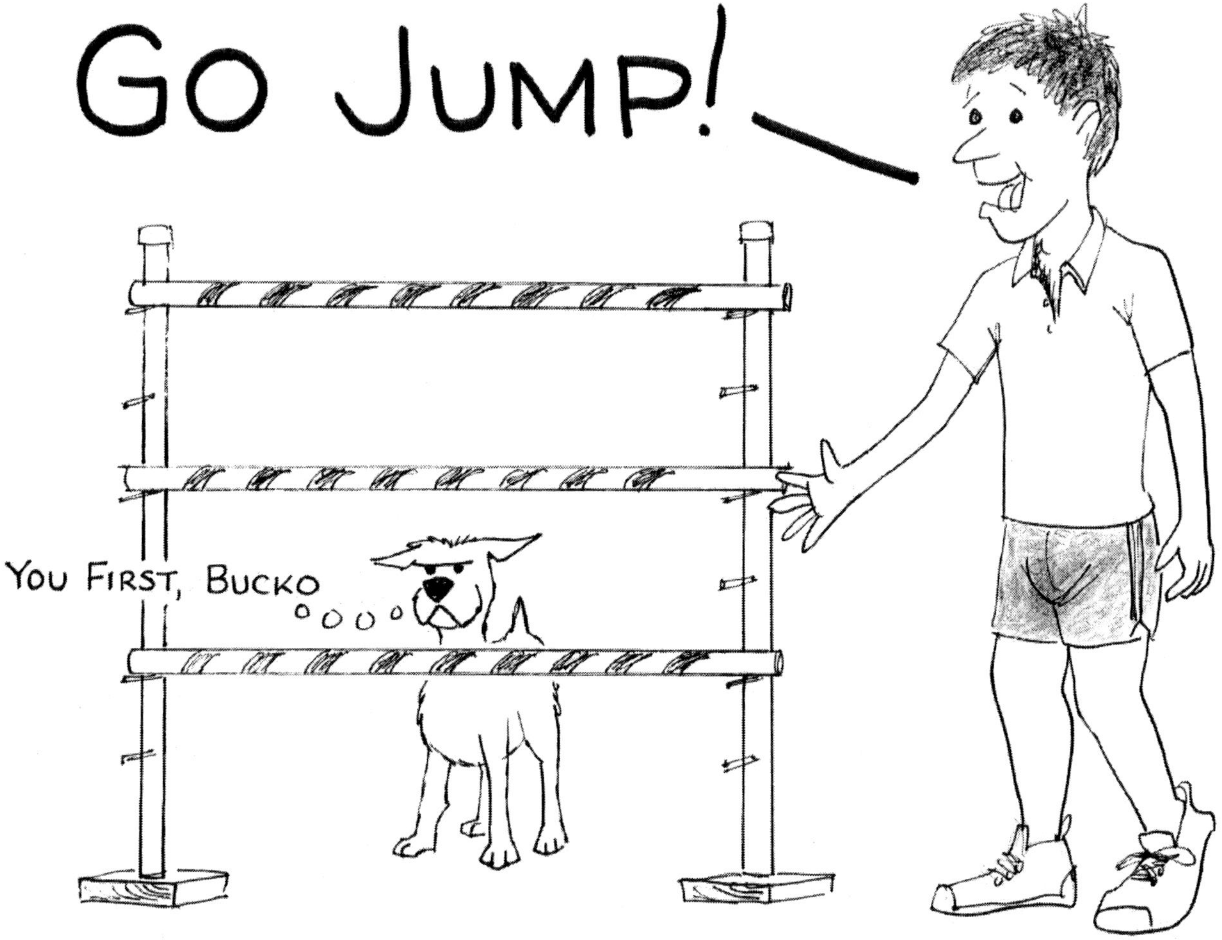
GO JUMP!
YOU FIRST, BUCKO

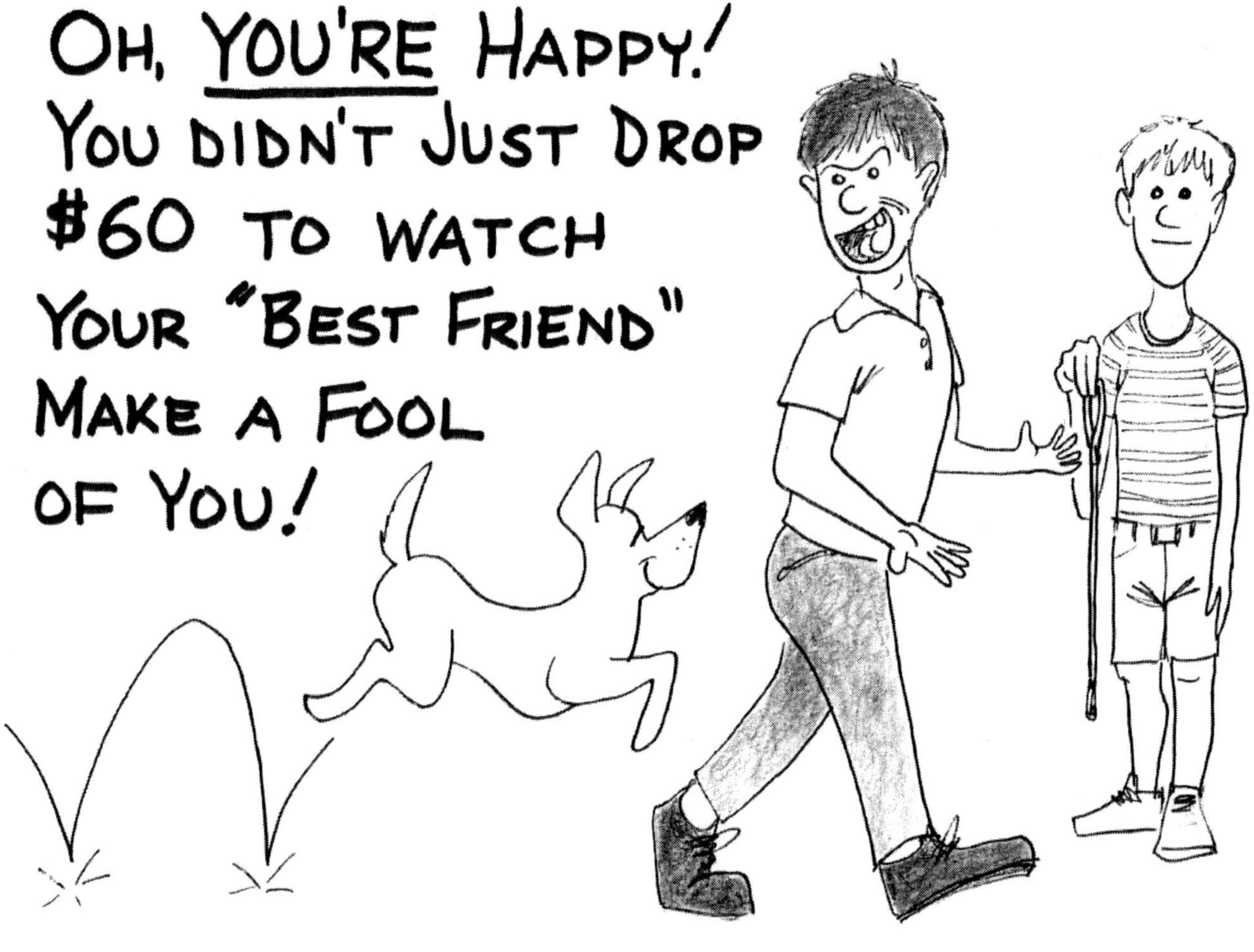
OH, YOU'RE HAPPY!
YOU DIDN'T JUST DROP
$60 TO WATCH
YOUR "BEST FRIEND"
MAKE A FOOL
OF YOU!

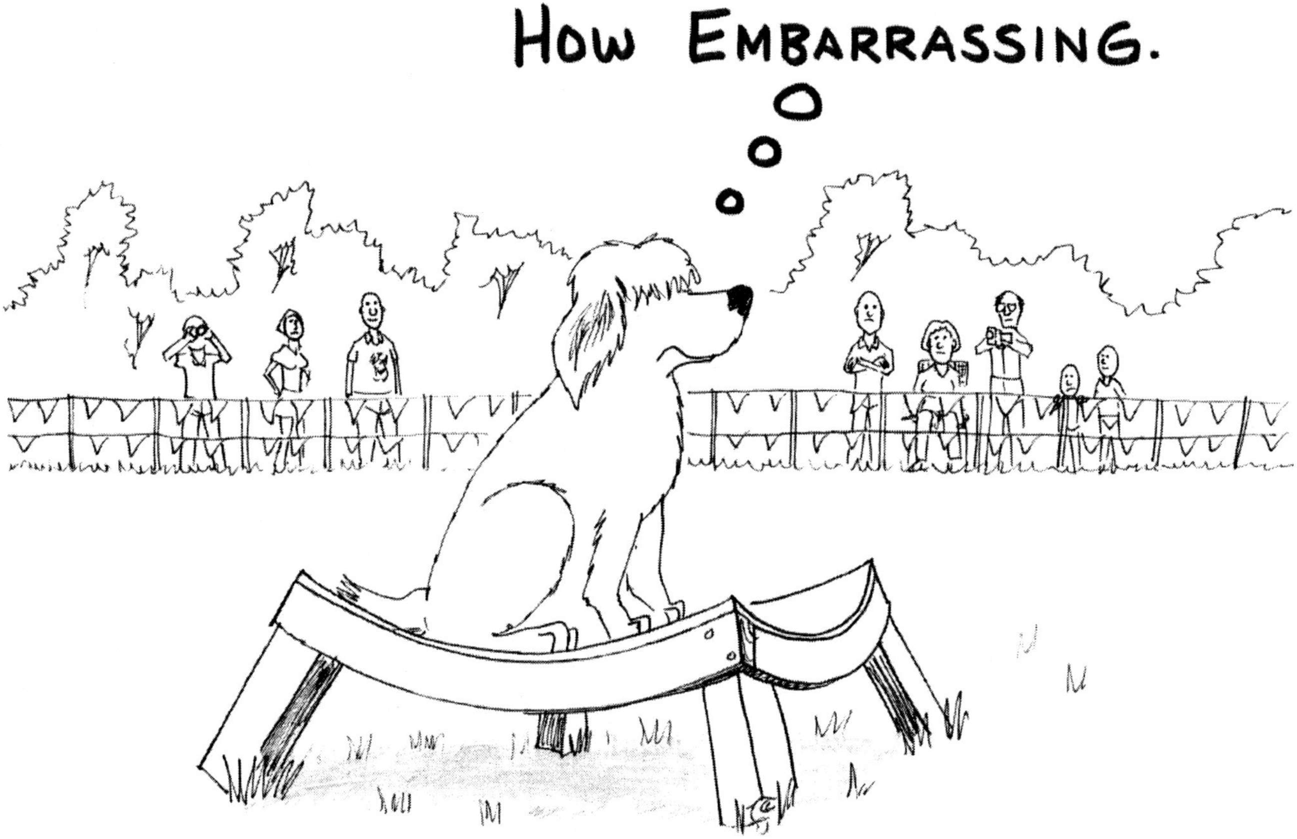
HOW EMBARRASSING.

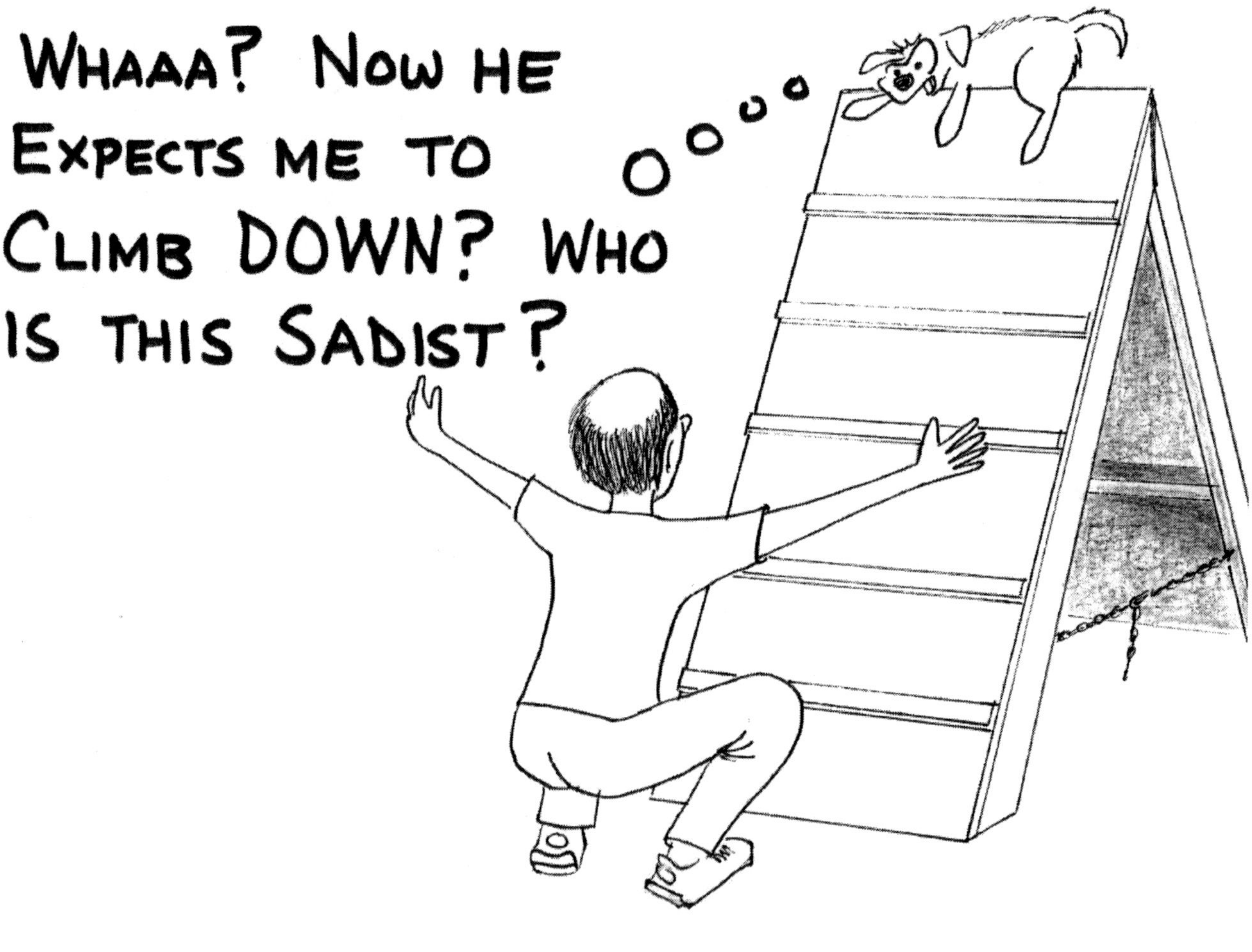
WHAAA? NOW HE EXPECTS ME TO CLIMB DOWN? WHO IS THIS SADIST?

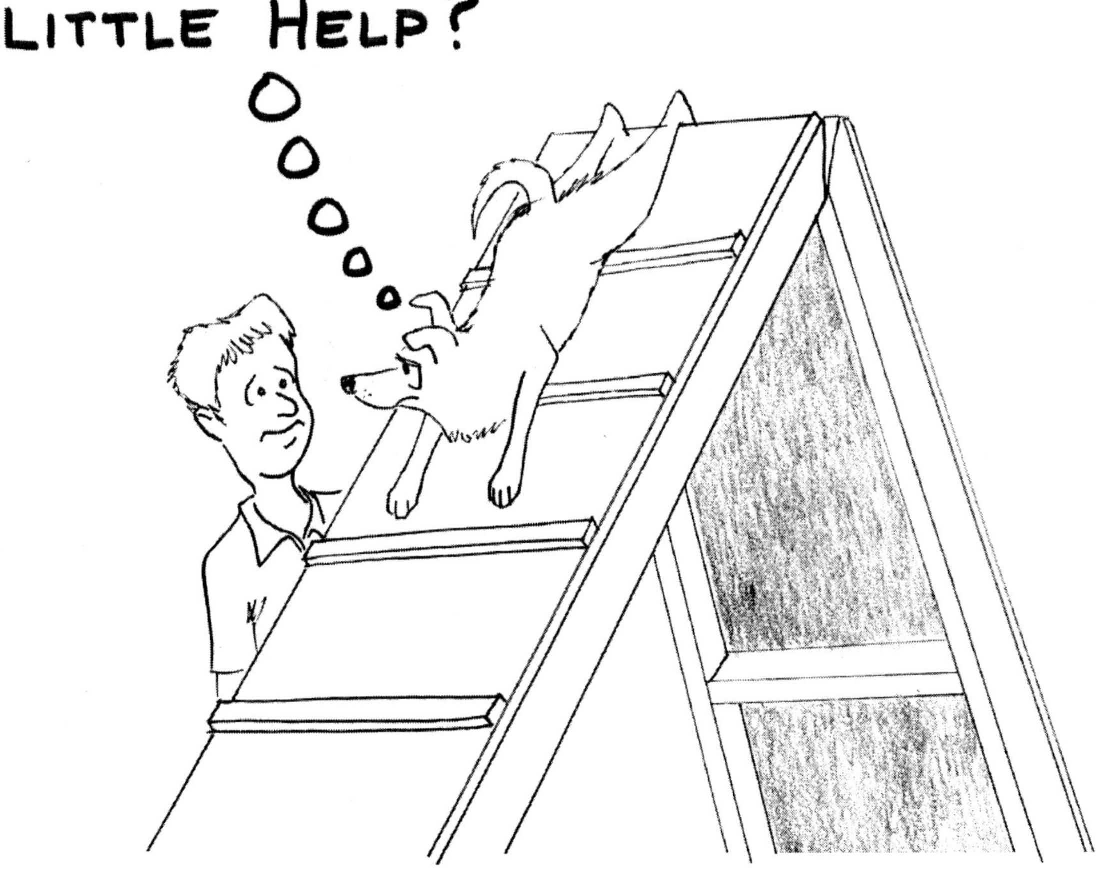
LITTLE HELP?

ONE OF THESE IS A QUALIFYING RIBBON; THE OTHER IS A PICKUP BAG. I ONLY WANT TO BE HANDED ONE OF THESE WHEN WE LEAVE THE RING.

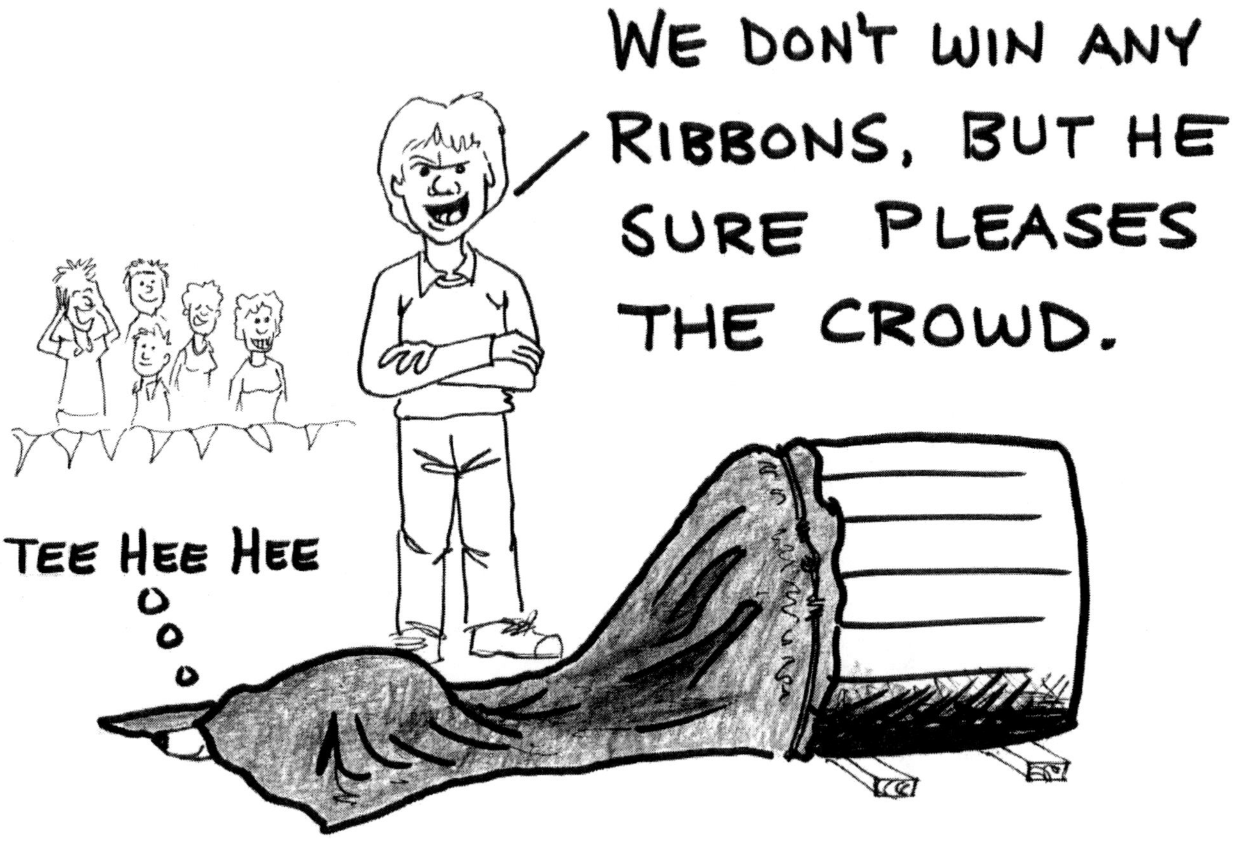
WE DON'T WIN ANY RIBBONS, BUT HE SURE PLEASES THE CROWD.
TEE HEE HEE

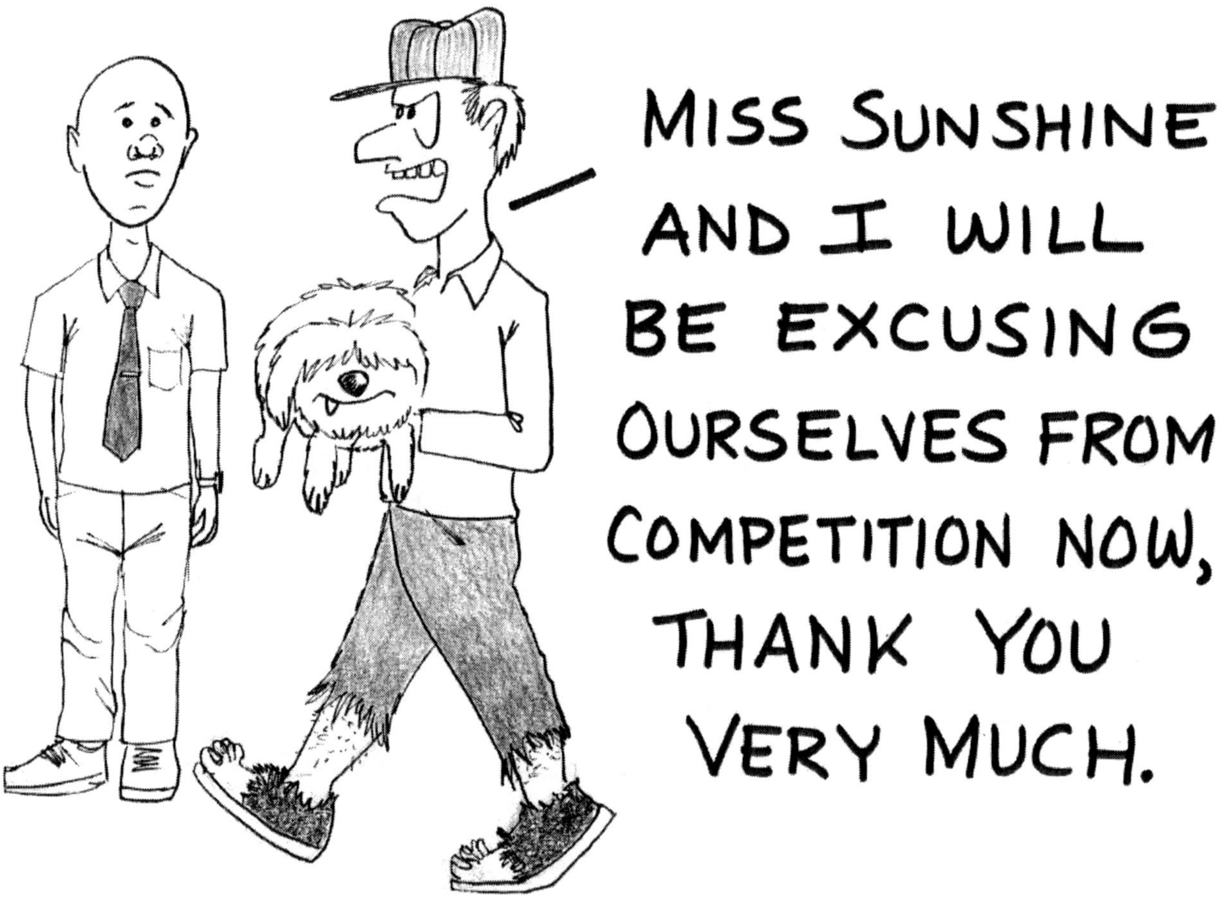
MISS SUNSHINE AND I WILL BE EXCUSING OURSELVES FROM COMPETITION NOW, THANK YOU VERY MUCH.

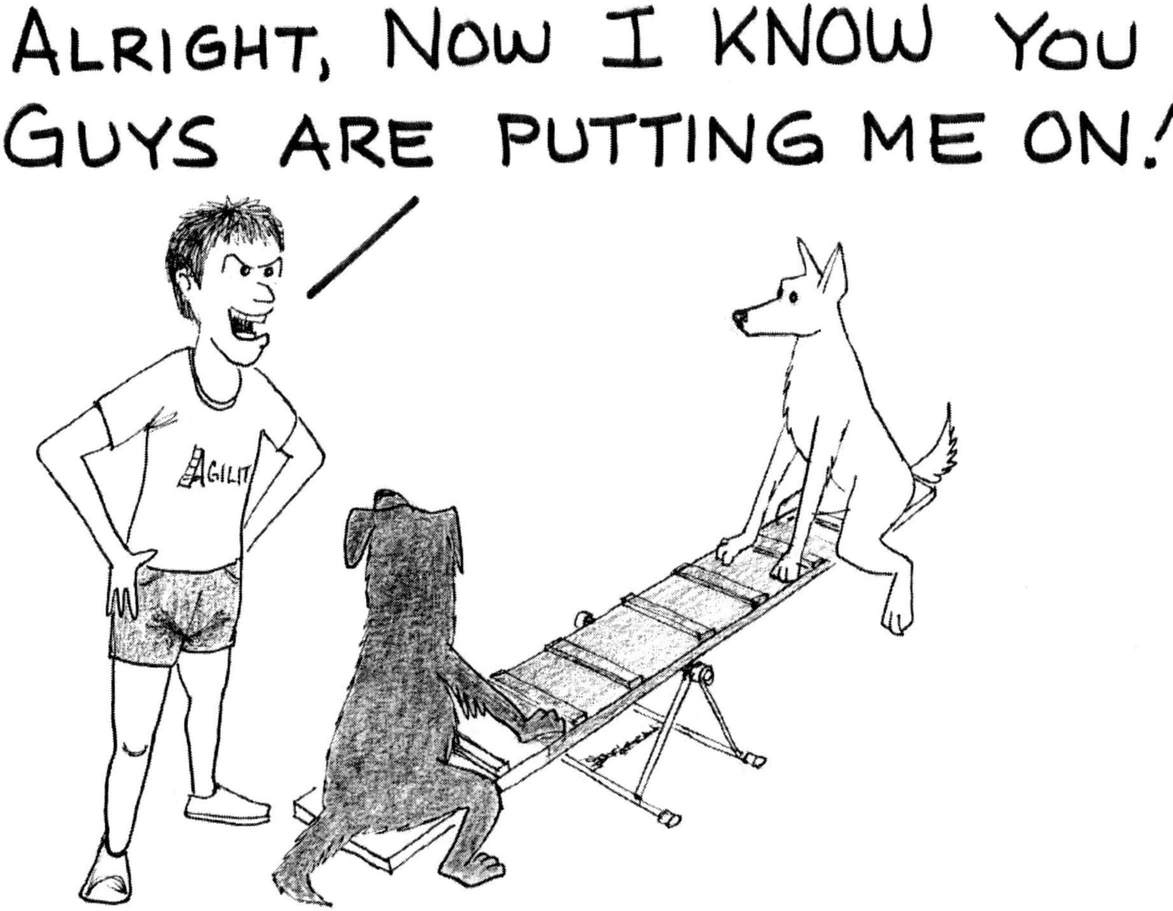
ALRIGHT, NOW I KNOW YOU GUYS ARE PUTTING ME ON!

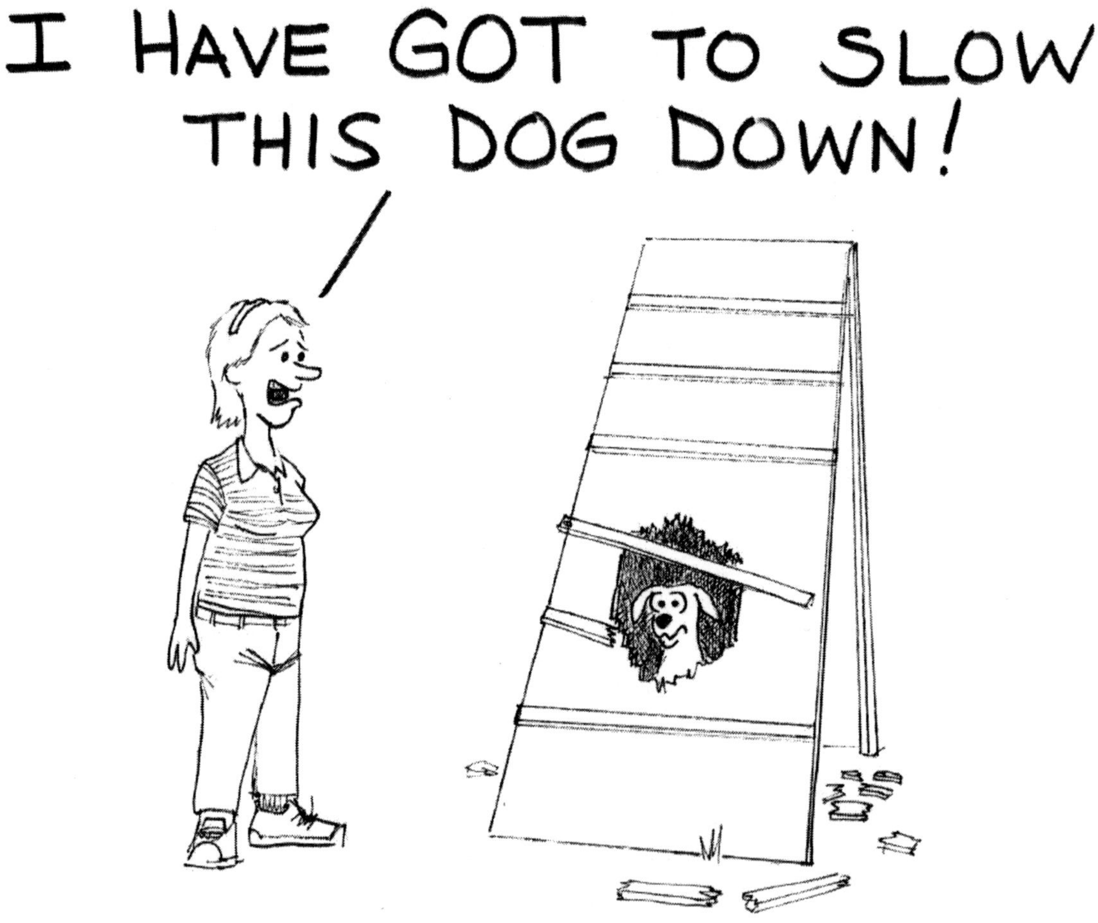
I HAVE GOT TO SLOW THIS DOG DOWN!

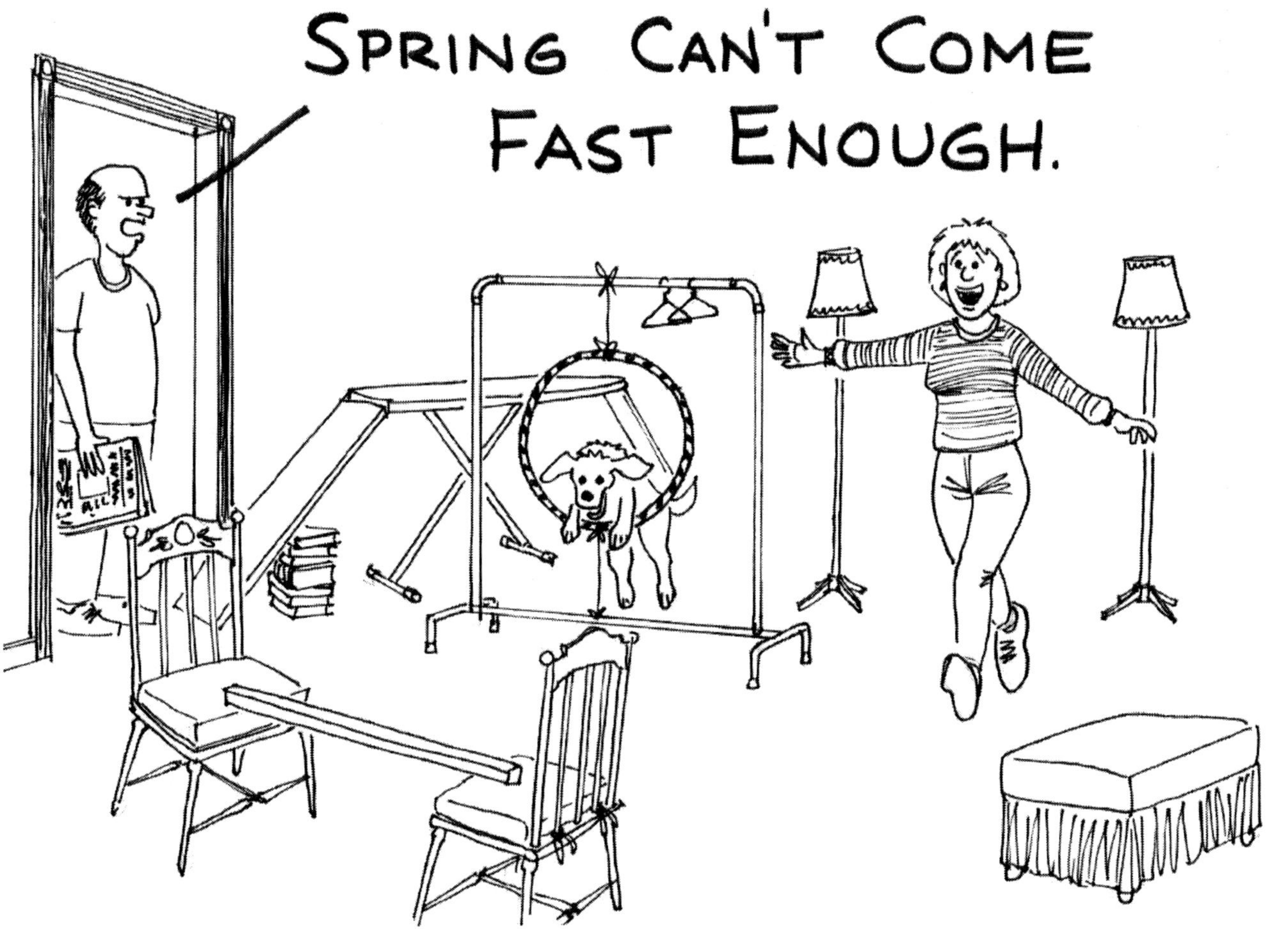
SPRING CAN'T COME FAST ENOUGH.

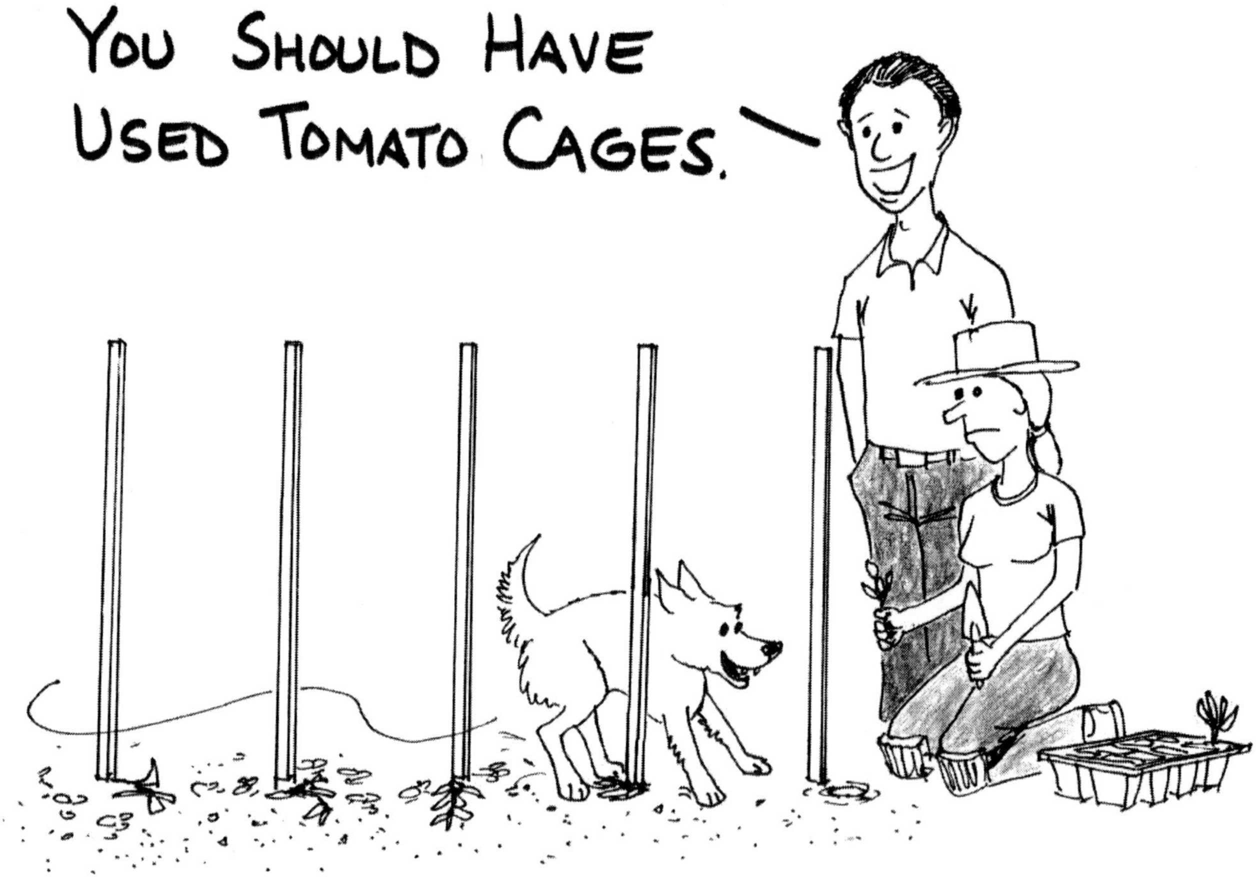
YOU SHOULD HAVE USED TOMATO CAGES.

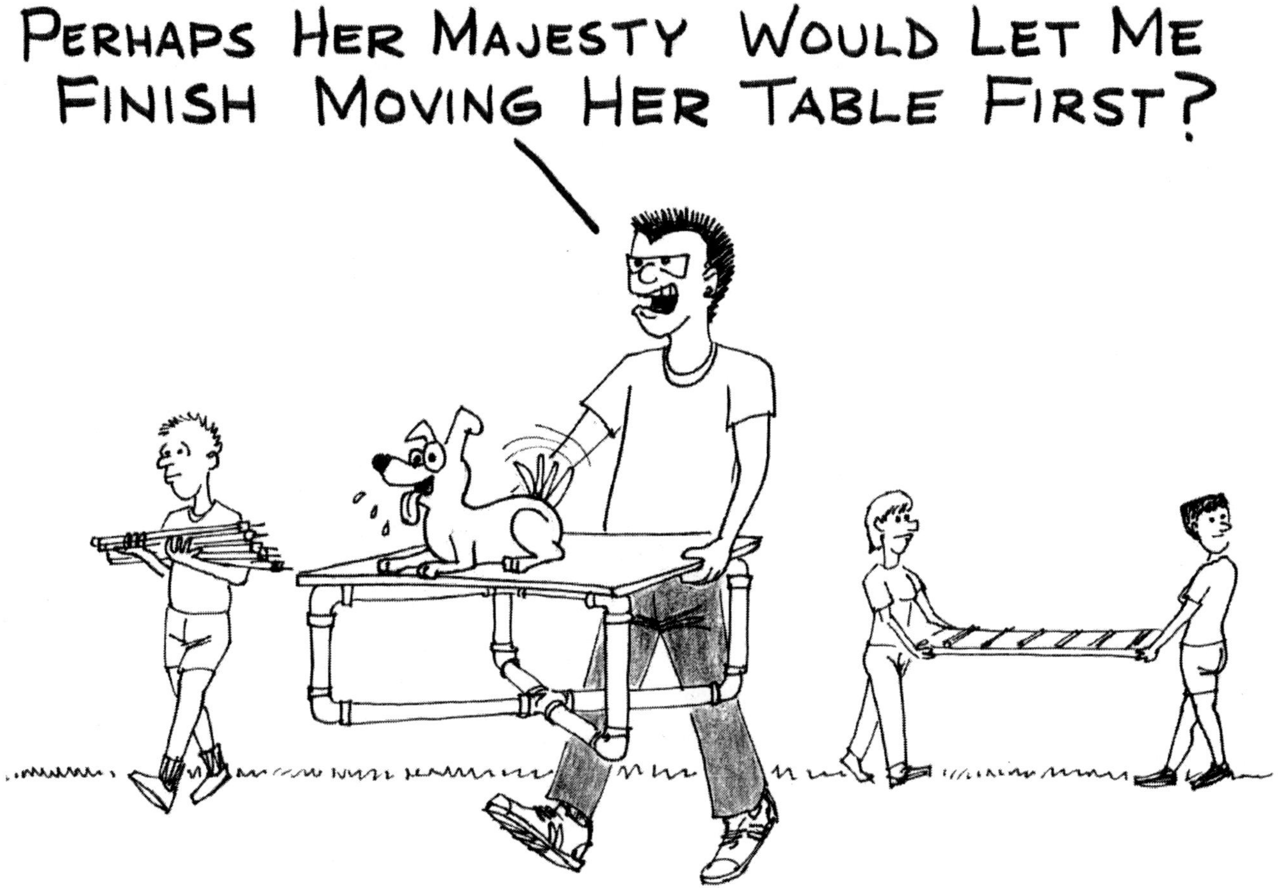
PERHAPS HER MAJESTY WOULD LET ME FINISH MOVING HER TABLE FIRST?

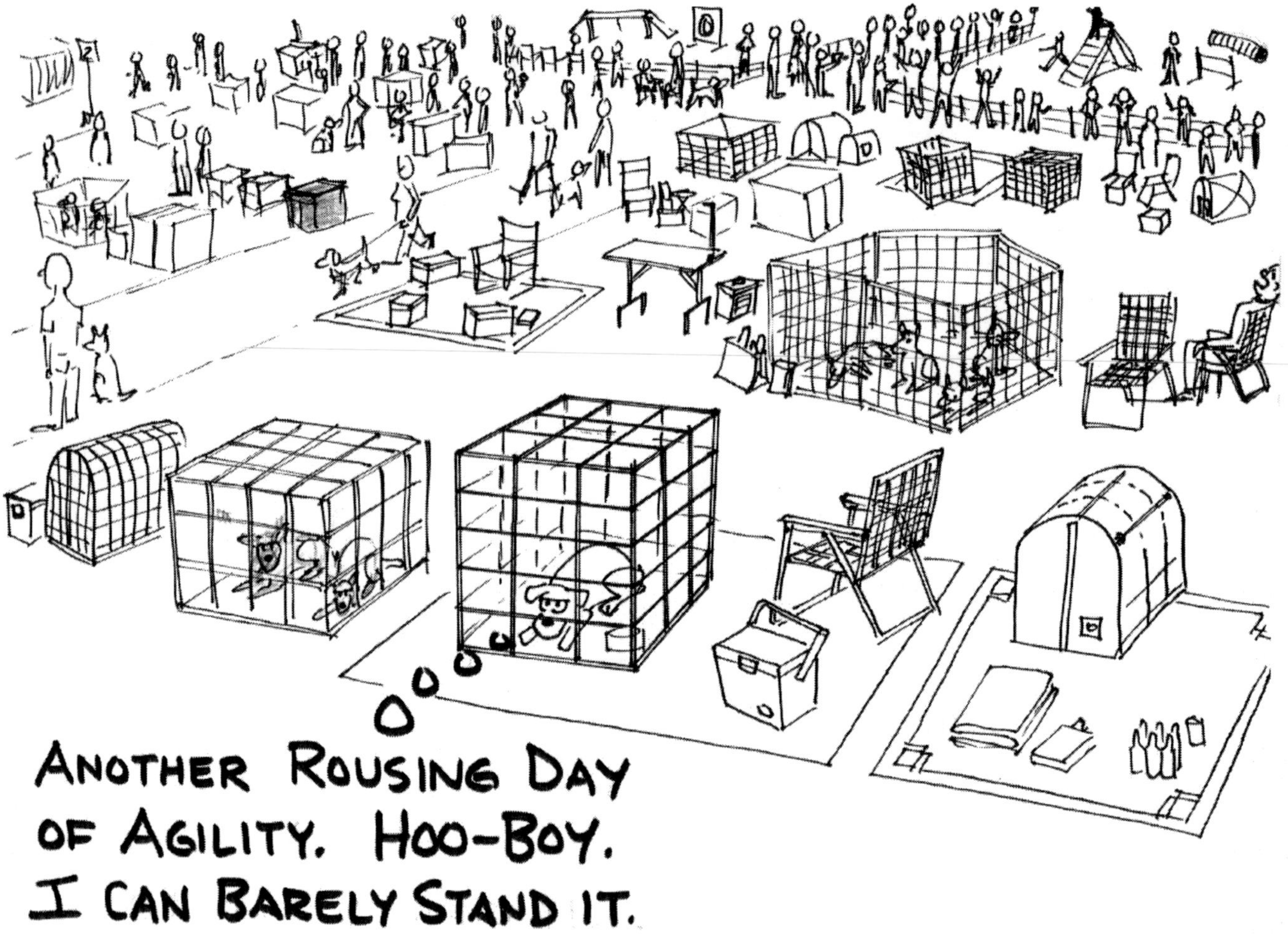
ANOTHER ROUSING DAY
OF AGILITY. HOO-BOY.
I CAN BARELY STAND IT.

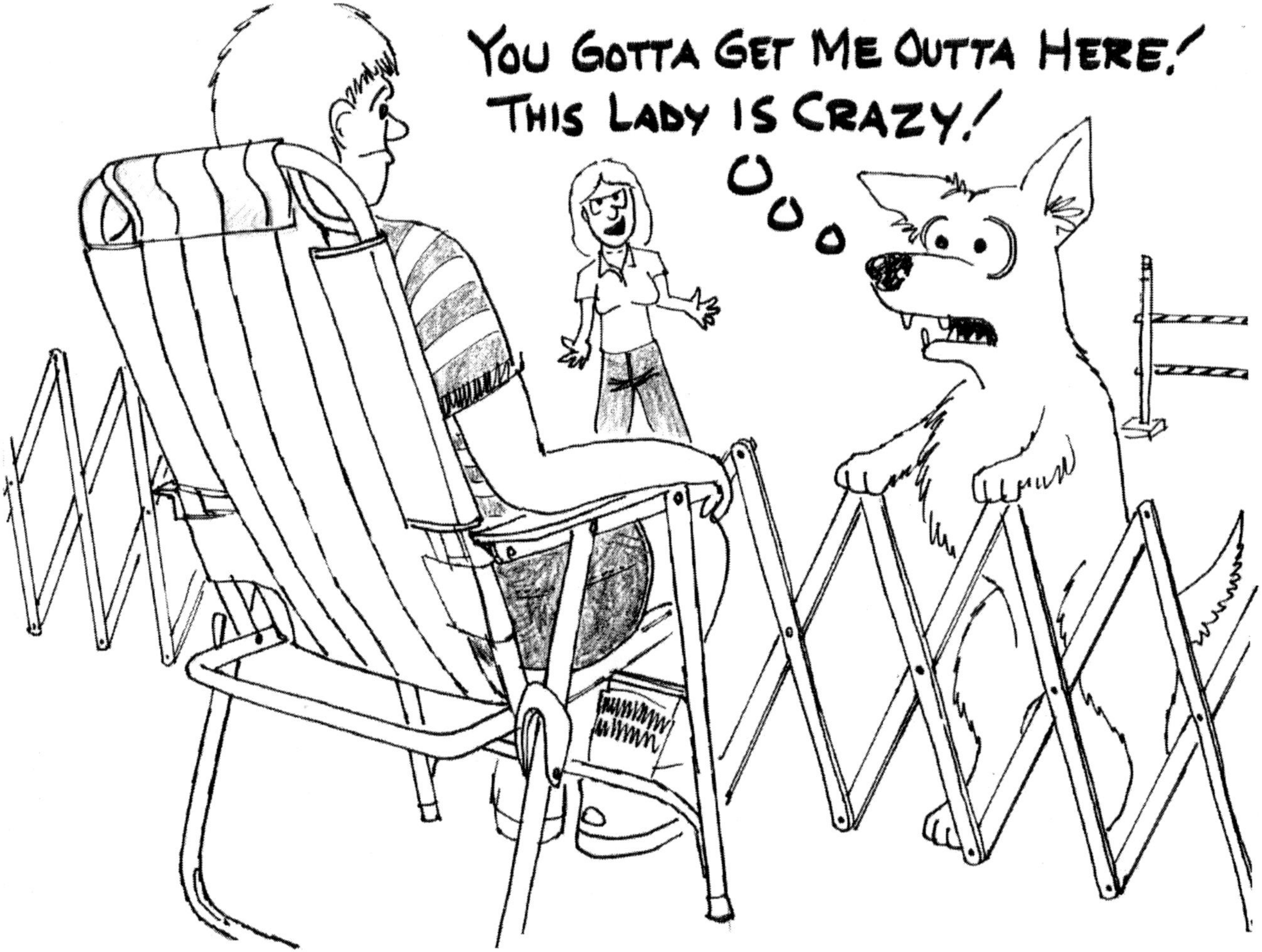
YOU GOTTA GET ME OUTTA HERE!
THIS LADY IS CRAZY!

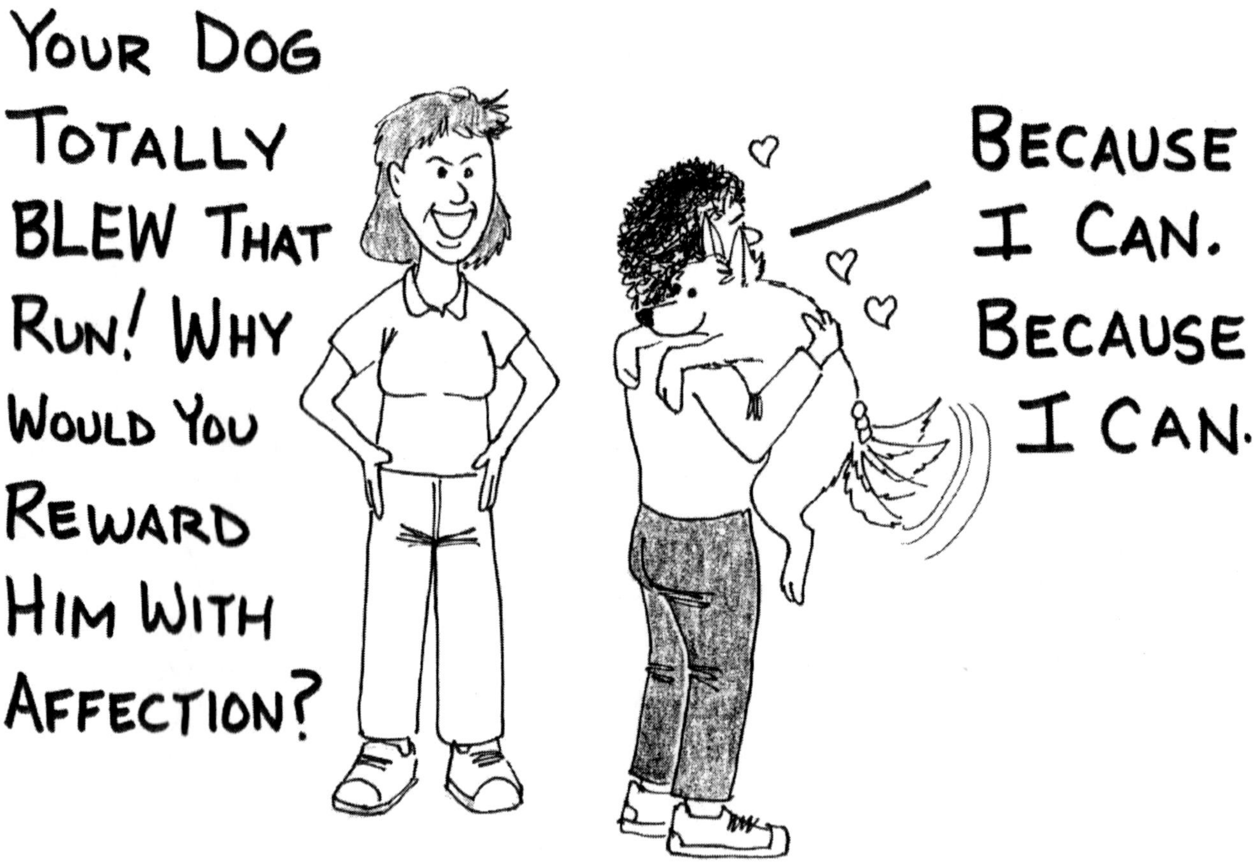
YOUR DOG TOTALLY BLEW THAT RUN! WHY WOULD YOU REWARD HIM WITH AFFECTION?
BECAUSE I CAN. BECAUSE I CAN.